No Ashes

R.C. Pace: A Sheriff's Life

By Katherine Anne Baldwin

Chapel Hill Press, Inc.
600 Franklin Square
1829 E. Franklin Street
Chapel Hill, NC 27514

ISBN Number 1-880849-39-9

Library of Congress Number 2001096175

Manufactured in the United States of America
04 03 02 01 10 9 8 7 6 5 4 3 2 1

Cover and book design by Molly Windsor

For my son, Tai Chun Yang

Acknowledgements

This book would not have been possible without the kind assistance of many people. First, the sons and daughters of R.C. Pace, their spouses and children, gave generously of their time for interviews. I was also given access to many photos, newspapers clippings, and other memorabilia that assisted my work enormously. In addition, the following people were interviewed:

W.D. Baldwin
Dr. Joe Dickerson
Dr. Arthur Miller
Estus Miller
R.C. Powell
C.R. "Poog" Smith
Dorothy Pace Smith
Arthur Stott
Joe Tonahill
Warren Woods

The Jasper County Historical Society Archives provided enormous assistance in research. Much of my documentation comes from the Jasper Newsboy, which serves as a valuable record of the life of Jasper County.

Nida Marshall graciously shared an interview with Beulah Pace Eddy from the 1970s which described the early childhood of the Pace children in Peachtree.

The Library of the Texas Rangers Hall of Fame kindly provided me with information on several Texas Rangers mentioned in this book.

Laura Leeah Overturf read my book in early versions and gave me excellent editorial advice.

Finally, my husband, Rod Knight, encouraged and supported me on many levels as I struggled to complete this book at the same time we were busy adopting (and now raising) our son from China.

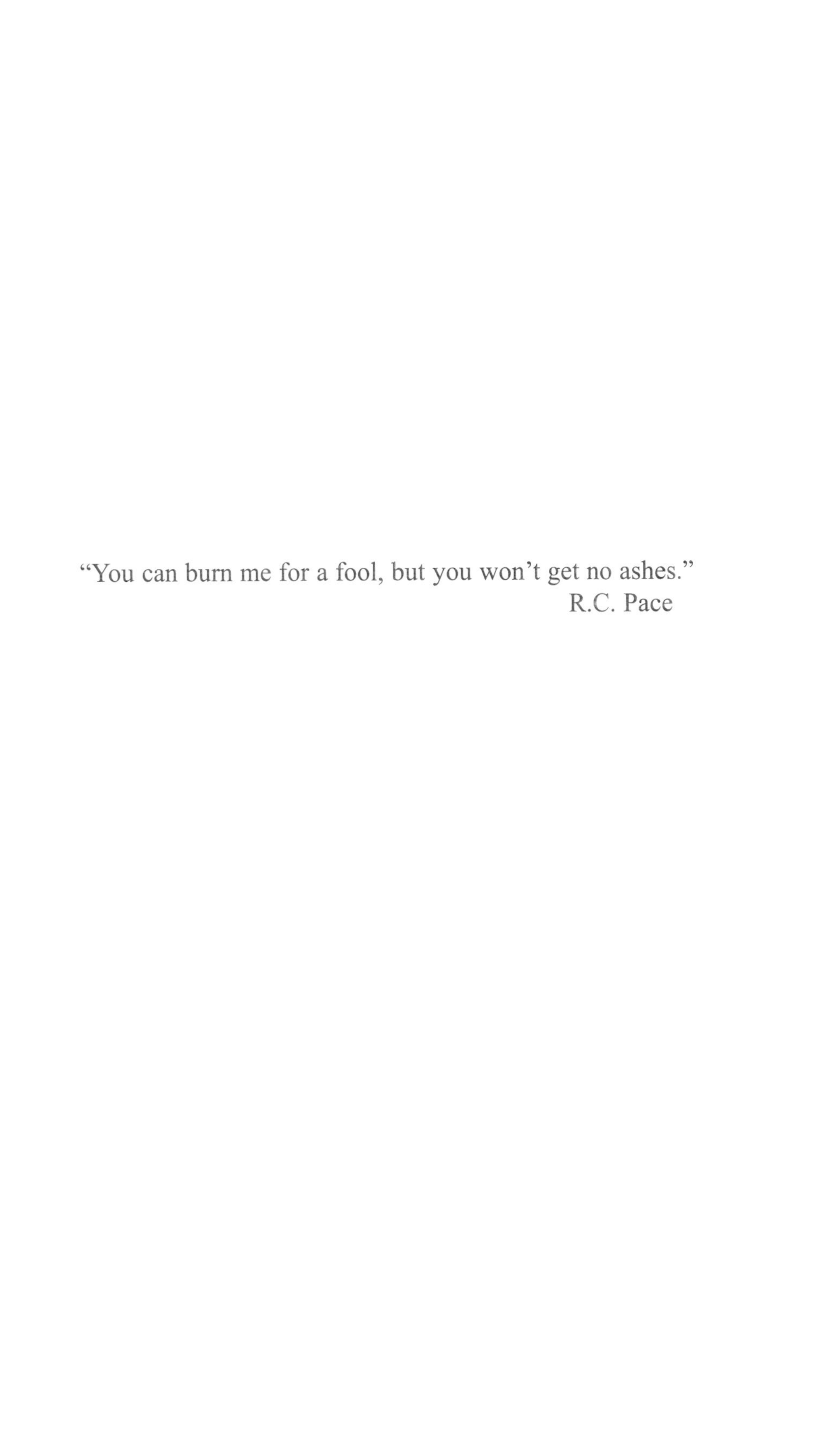

"You can burn me for a fool, but you won't get no ashes."
R.C. Pace

Introduction

Jasper County is in the heart of what is known as the Piney Woods of Texas. For non-Texans, it is not the wide, flat, cactus-dotted prairie that is the Texas of one's imagination. It is a dense forest with steep hills. Bordered in part by the Neches River, it was, in the 1800s, sparsely populated and a better place to hunt and fish than to make a living. Except for a population burst during the big timber push from the late 1800s to the 1930s, when sawmill towns expanded (later to disappear), the growth in the area has been fairly slow.

For all its hardship, it was a popular place for the first settlers who arrived in the 1820s. Unlike Central Texas, the Piney Woods had friendly native tribes. Farming was good here, especially cotton. Outbreaks of disease were common - malaria and yellow fever in particular - but the families who arrived, mostly stayed. Generations of locals descended from the intermarriage of a few dozen families whose names recur in census after census.

The idea for this book began when I acquired my grandfather's old trunk a few years ago. It revealed his work life as a sheriff: notes on crimes, photos of murder scenes, threatening letters. This discovery led to my wanting to know about the work life of the man who, to me, had been a wonderful grandfather, but something of a mystery as a sheriff. To me, R.C. Pace was the anchor that held the Paces together. He and his wife welcomed their grandchildren into their home, and many nights were spent sleeping upstairs in the bedrooms still decorated with our parents' things. He hunted with his grandsons and was entertained by his granddaughters' play. Once, he took me out to teach me how to milk a cow. I was about five or six years old, and he sat on the low wooden stool with me close by his side to observe. Then he pulled on the cow and squirted milk in my face! His laughter filled the air, making me forget the indignity and appreciate the man who was never afraid to have fun.

My interviews for this book took place over several years, although many of the family stories have been written on my heart from childhood. The stories I write are as accurate as time and memory will allow. Newspaper accounts of some events helped to verify names and some facts. The larger part of the stories were events in which only a few people were present. In those instances, or where several witnesses gave conflicting stories, I have had to settle for emotional truth – what was said and what was done describe my grandfather's ways and character, as recalled by those who loved him. This is the truth in a small town. Even an unproven rumor contains valuable information. Belief in a rumor is evidence of general public opinion, of reputation, and of the parameters of local experience or imagination.

The times during which my grandfather lived were rugged and often crude. Many of the people I interviewed look back fondly on them, and it is understandable. These were the glory days for many white men. They lived and ruled with impunity, so life was uncomplicated. Most of these people were comfortable with strict racial segregation. Women were the sturdy helpmates at home. There was little room for weakness in the harsh environment. Children were obedient because their chores left them little time for mischief. Attitudes and behaviors were not what might now be called "politically correct" or even constitutional, but that is how life was.

There is nostalgia for that, nowadays. People grow misty-eyed thinking about a sheriff who could clear the streets with a leather blackjack or stern look. There is a sort of community myth from about the 1950s forward that Jasper County was filled with well-behaved, church-going people who never locked their doors. Still, the good old days were not so good, and my research found that again and again. It was Sheriff R.C. Pace who saw the darker and meaner side of the town. As one person described it: "He didn't deal with Sunday school teachers, or even with those who went to Sunday school." He knew Jasper's secrets and dealt with the situations that other did not want to know even existed. Much of what he saw then is commonplace in today's news. Back then, scandalous details were told only in whispers. A sheriff had a unique burden that required special strengths. This book tells the story of how one man grew into that role.

1890

★ ★ ★ ★ ★

Chapter One

Hardy Allen Pace always said he wouldn't leave the family farm come hell or high water. But as he looked out over the dead and stunted remains of his cotton field, he knew that a drought had changed everything. Hardy grew cotton on several hundred acres in the Peachtree community in Jasper County. He had a wife and two children to support and he was desperate. It was time to leave so his family could survive.

It was the custom at that time for a local businessman to act as a patron to a farmer - extending loans and other assistance. Hardy contacted his patron, Nathan Hart. Mr. Hart quickly found work for Hardy in the timber business. At that time, East Texas was in the heat of the first big timber push and Hardy drove a team of oxen, felling virgin timber and dragging the logs to the Angelina River. The logs were floated downstream to the sawmill. It was backbreaking work, and the men stayed in a small cabin in the woods. Hardy's wife, Fannie, brought them their meals.

Mr. Hart next found work for Hardy in the nearby town of Colmesneil. The Paces packed up their belongings into a wagon and gave Lawrence, the family cat, to the neighbors. Their daughter, Beulah, was extremely fond of the cat - it had belonged to her grandmother, Mary Hancock Hall. The children had a life with few pleasures. She and her older brother Henry played with spools that their mother had given them when she had used up the thread for hand sewing. Leaving the cat was almost unbearable for her. As they rode away from their farm, she saw Lawrence in the road and began screaming hysterically, "That's my cat! That's my cat!" Her parents calmed her down and they rode on to Tyler

County, where Fannie took in boarders and her husband worked as a timekeeper at the timber mill. On January 16, 1891, she gave birth to their last child, Robert Carroll Pace. He would be known as R.C. his entire life.

The family moved back to Peachtree as soon as they had some money saved. Pay was good, and Hardy bought his wife her first sewing machine. Back on the farm, all three children learned the survival skills necessary for farm life. Education was clearly valued as well; records show they attended local schools through the high school level. Hardy briefly considered moving out to West Texas as many of his neighbors were doing. He took his horse and rode west several hundred miles to look around. When he returned, he told the family, "There is land out there for seventy-five cents an acre, and good farm land for a dollar. But I just didn't have the dollar!"

After the turn of the century, Hardy gave up farm life and moved to the county seat of Jasper, where he served as county clerk. His wife raised a big garden and took care of the family. Their oldest son, Henry, worked on farms and learned carpentry. Beulah preferred her father's work. She often went along to his office and helped him with his duties. Young R.C. enjoyed a close relationship with his older siblings, but when he was thirteen, tragedy struck.

One day R.C. asked Henry to take some corn to the gristmill for grinding. Henry was always happy to oblige his little brother and took his horse down to the mill on Indian Creek. It was winter, and there had been a lot of rain. On the way home, the horse got balky in some mud. Henry had a bit of fiery temperament that could have been Pace, or could have been Hall, like his mother. He ended up getting thrown from the horse into the mud. By the time he finally got home, his clothes were frozen to his body.

Henry, now twenty, had enjoyed some lucky breaks before in his life. He had stayed well when a younger brother, Charlie, died at the age of two from malaria. At sixteen, he worked in Galveston, but left two weeks before the massive Hurricane of 1900 destroyed the island and took thousands of lives. He could not outrun pneumonia though, and perished within weeks. The year was 1904.

Henry's death was the first in a series of tragedies for the Pace family. Hardy soon learned that he suffered from stomach cancer. In those days, there were no treatments of any use, but many people flocked to the town of Mineral Wells, where the waters and the doctors were thought to be helpful. Hardy visited there, as well. Foreseeing that his life would be short, he sought to set up his wife in a large boarding house in downtown Jasper. Beulah took teacher training and worked for a while as a teacher. Hardy wrote often from his visits to Mineral Wells, and one surviving letter reveals a deep concern for his family:

Windsor Hotel *Feb. 28, 1909*

Dear RC and Beulah,

Your letter and card of the 26th received today. Was sorry to hear Momma was suffering with cough and cold. Hope she is better by this time. If she does not get better, write me at once, and if any of you get sick much, wire me because it seems I cannot get a letter from home for under two or three days. Beulah's letter of the 24th was received on the 25th. If all of them would come through that way, I could start home on a return train in case it was necessary.

I am feeling very well today - better than I have since I came here. I was feeling very bad yesterday and thought of seeing a doctor but if I keep mending don't know that I will consult a doctor at all but a few more days like yesterday and I will have a doctor or hit the road home. That medicine I wrote you about I believe has been a help to me.

He continued with some career advice to his son:

R.C. you said you could get the house from Jim Smith but had not fully decided what you would do yet. What you want to do is [find out] what the business will cost to start. That is what the outfit will cost. Then figure on rent and the amount of business as near as you can. If you decide not to go into that business I hope you can get something to do in order to help bear expenses.

I wish you would see the old man Jefferson and tell him I am here and in need of that $20 if it is possible for him to get it. If you succeed in getting it, keep it until I have to send for some money, which I hope I will not have to do. There is several little debts I can't recall now and several deeds on which the recording fees are due and if you can collect them you may have all you can collect. But that part of it you want to keep.

Some of you try to take time and write me every day so I may know all is well, or not well, as the case may be. Hoping these few words may reach and find Mama better and all the rest. Your Papa

Hardy died three months later.

Following the death of his father, R.C. began training as a carpenter. He found work with a local builder, Mr. Cook, who taught a variety of skills to the young man. Family memory is that R.C. took additional training in a school north of Jasper County at San Augustine. The school offered classes in mathematics that R.C. needed for his work. One of R.C.'s daughters recalls that he told her with a laugh he was thrown out of the school for stealing a test.

Mr. Cook impressed young R.C. with his wisdom, as well as his business sense. The man was a shrewd observer and diplomatic in the way he handled people. Cook was approached for jobs by many people. He always spoke kindly to them. If they were too unskilled for his needs, Cook told them he was not hiring anyone. One time, R.C. heard Cook insist he was not hiring at a time that workers were in fact needed. When R.C. asked, "What did you tell him a lie for?" Cook replied, " I didn't want to hurt his feelings - I'd rather have the good will of a dog rather than the ill will of him."

R.C. became an eager student in the art of dealing with people. Mr. Cook also cultivated new talent and skills. When someone arrived in town with a new skill or way of building, Cook hired them quickly. It was a time of rapid change and Cook knew the importance of learning the latest methods. In many ways, Cook served R.C. well as a mentor, and they continued working together for several years.

His career as a carpenter was postponed with the outbreak of World War I. An excellent horseman, R.C. was natural for the infantry. His carpentry skills made him more useful as a mechanic. He sailed to Europe and served from Sept. 1917 until June 1919. His discharge papers describe him as 26 years old with blue eyes and brown hair, six feet tall when he enlisted.

Many people forget that the Spanish Flu epidemic killed more people than the war, and R.C. witnessed its effects. He was sick in Europe but recovered in a way that is somewhat disputed in the family.

One of his sons recalls that R.C. had the flu. His helpfulness to the cooks in his military unit caused them to share lemons with him for making a hot lemon drink. The son remembers R.C. "swore and be damned" that the lemons were the key to his recovery. But one of his daughters remembered otherwise. In her version, R.C. wanted lemons from the Red Cross, but they tried to charge him money for them. When the Salvation Army came along, they gave him the lemons for free. She insists he always held a low opinion of the Red Cross for this reason.

In any case, he survived the war intact. He did have one adventure that became a favorite family tale. He and another soldier, an Indian from Oklahoma, supposedly went out one night on a bender. They barricaded themselves in a man's wine cellar and proceeded to drink their way out. This landed them both in the brig. R.C. managed to gain release, but the Indian tried to strangle a first lieutenant through the bars of the cell, and was held for court-martial.

R.C. soon left Europe for the hard trip home. He later told his children about the rough journey by sea. He said that the troops were low on food and had to eat horsemeat. One of the other soldiers joked, "It's bad enough having to eat this damn mule, but they could at least skin him first!"

The war was not the only hardship R.C.'s family suffered in those years. His sister Beulah married soon after their father died in 1909. She had two young sons when her husband, Zim Eddy, died of pneumonia in 1917.

When R.C. returned from the war, the country was undergoing tremendous change. His life would take a new direction, as well.

1919

★★★★★

Chapter Two

With the war behind him, R.C. tried to rebuild his life quickly. His mother had a boarding house that provided her with a modest living, but he wanted to get on his feet and help take responsibility for her and his sister. He was twenty-eight, and the small town of Jasper did not offer him the opportunity he sought, but another town did.

R.C. went to the oilfield boomtown of Burkburnett, Texas. There, in the western part of the state, he built camp housing for the workers. He was able to save his money, and after a year or so, was ready to return home to live the life he knew, working, hunting, and helping to raise his two nephews. He used his savings to buy an early model Ford and a pack of hounds and came back to Jasper.

R.C. had excellent skills and experience as a carpenter, but when he returned to Jasper, he turned to a completely new field - law enforcement. He was hired as a deputy for one of Jasper's most notorious sheriffs, Beaver Bishop. Beaver Bishop grew up in Jasper County and is remembered to have been a lively child. When he was small he spent time with different relatives. He was easily drawn to mischief. Once he and some cousins were playing on a porch where bales of raw cotton were stored. In the course of their play, the cotton caught fire and everyone scrambled to put it out. Afterward, Beaver was quick to brag, "Aunt Mat, if I hadn't of been here, your place woulda burnt up, wouldn't it?" He was happy to be a hero, even though he probably had started the fire.

Beaver's entire life paralleled that attitude of the boastful, yet mischievous, child. He was vigorous in breaking up illegal moonshine operations throughout the county. This was the beginning of Prohibition. There is also a wide opinion that he ran his own stills or protected some who did. Several of his deputies were known for unregulated meanness, particularly against the black community. One person described Bishop's reputation for "killing blacks for frivolous reasons" and even a Bishop family member says he killed eleven people while sheriff.

In some ways, he was a larger-than-life character with the strengths and weaknesses that have been seen in or attributed to most Jasper sheriffs. He stood six feet seven, and there was no doubt he was tough. Once a man came to the jail to alert R.C. that a local bootlegger was gunning for Beaver. The man went on at some length about how hard the bootlegger was searching. Finally, R.C. just smiled and said, "Naww, that ain't the way it is a-tall! He KNOWS where Beaver Bishop is and he DAMNED sure don't want to find him!"

Bishop did have considerable success in destroying stills. On one famous occasion, he brought barrels of moonshine to the courthouse square, pulled out his pistol, and shot them full of holes. This drew a number of citizens to scoop up the moonshine in their hats as it poured out into the street! A less publicized event occurred among family. He once found some stills near a relative's farm. He brought the barrels over to the farm and fed the corn liquor to the hogs. The hogs got drunk and rolled in the mud until they sobered up. Then they drank even more. It fattened them up, too!

Beaver was a tall and striking ladies' man who got married late in life to Dess Mae Stephenson. The Stephensons were a long-time Texas family from Orange County on the Texas coast. Beaver and Mae had one son.

Around 1920, a niece came to live with them. Jessie Viva Linscome trained as a nurse and worked in Galveston. Her mother (the sister of Dess Mae Bishop) had recently died and Viva had come to Jasper to recover from scarlet fever. She quickly found work as a nurse for local doctors in the rural community. She was a short woman with dark hair and intense eyes that hinted of the Cajun ancestry on her father's side. She was from a large family with five sisters; she later said that her sisters considered her an "old maid" at eighteen. It was clear that finding a husband was not on her list of priorities.

Jasper was a rugged place at that time. There were frequent epidemics of malaria and other deadly illnesses in this time before effective antibiotics. Sawmill work was extremely dangerous and injuries were common. The town had few doctors, and Viva was kept busy with work.

The social upheaval that led to Prohibition also gave rise to another group movement at that time in Texas: the resurgence of the Ku Klux Klan. Fueled by a large wave of new immigrants from Europe, and a desire to return to a past that was moral and orderly, the Klan grew rapidly. The organization claimed to stand for this return to traditional morality. Historical accounts tell of Klan crusades against drinking, marital infidelity, immoral movies, and wife beating. East Texas newspaper accounts reported tar and featherings of several whites for these offenses. The victims were described as a woman accused of bigamy, a Beaumont doctor who performed abortions, and a Deweyville man who took a woman to the same doctor. In 1921, there were 100,000 Klan members in Texas.

R.C. Pace was briefly caught up in this crusade. He joined the Klan, and for some years his membership card and Klan robe were packed away in an old trunk at his home. He never spoke of it later to any of his children, and it is thought that he lost interest, as many in Texas did, after a few years. The Klan robe disappeared before the children were grown.

The excesses of the group became increasingly violent and indiscriminate. Texas Rangers were called in for a Klan riot near Waco in 1921. Viva Linscome lost an uncle, George Stephenson, to the Klan in 1924. George was out tending his cattle one day near Deweyville when he saw a car pass. Inside were some Klansmen and a tar-and-feathering victim. When the authorities asked him about it later, George admitted that he knew the identity of the people in the car. He readily agreed to testify in a trial against the Klansmen. George had a history of being in gunfights, and Viva's mother was described by one neighbor as being "the meanest white woman he ever knew." Before George Stephenson had the chance to identify the men in court, however, neighbors found him dead in his field. He had been shot in the back.

A man like R.C., who certainly enjoyed a drink, was in peculiar company with a group so closely aligned with the temperance movement. The simple answer that he was attracted to the group's racism because of his own beliefs, does not seem accurate by itself. He was a deputy, and needed no robe and hood if he wanted to beat up black people in the county. Perhaps it was the other goals of the group - taking a stand for moral behavior – that were appealing. The group regularly railed against wife-beaters, a type of criminal R.C. particularly disliked. It may have been that he was drawn into the group because of its popularity with other men whom he admired. The size of the Klan in Texas gave it considerable political influence, and that may have interested him. In any case, the affiliation did not last for long, and his work as a deputy kept him busy. The county was booming with sawmill towns and all sorts of lawlessness.

1921

★ ★ ★ ★ ★

Chapter Three

The family legend goes something like this: R.C. walked into a dance one night and saw Viva Linscome. He turned to a friend and said, "That's the woman I'm going to marry." His easy confidence in his work, however, didn't translate well to romantic endeavors. They went out on occasion, but Viva was less than enthusiastic and continued to date others. She told later how one of R.C.'s friends teased her, "Viva, when are you going to marry R.C. and make a MAN out of him?" But she remained quite content with her work.

After about a year, R.C. invited her to ride with him to the tiny community of Wiergate on some business. On the ride back, he said, "Viva, why the hell won't you go with me?" To which she responded, "Well, R.C., you never asked me!"

Some time after, Viva prepared to take a bus to Beaumont, where she had a date with another man. She stopped at the courthouse first, dressed in a nice traveling suit. R.C. was there. They walked together in the courthouse hallway and he excused himself to speak for a moment with the local judge. The two men emerged from the judge's office and continued along. R.C. made sure that the judge carried his book with him. Suddenly, R.C. stopped at the clerk's office and announced, "We'd like to buy a marriage license!" Too stunned to refuse, Viva agreed, and the two were married on the spot! The date was November 22, 1922. When she later went back to her aunt to tell her what had happened, Aunt Mae replied, "If he'd given you five minutes, you would have turned him down!"

If R.C. had difficulties with Beaver Bishop's style of law enforcement, the marriage resolved them. Due to rules against nepotism, he could not continue to work for his wife's uncle, so he had married himself out of a job. Viva was most likely relieved to move away from the Bishop home, where there was well-known marital discord. Beaver had a reputation as a womanizer and even gave his wife a venereal disease. This illness (at a time before antibiotics), or her own private turmoil, contributed to Mae Stephenson's emotional deterioration. She eventually spent some time in the state mental hospital at Rusk. Their son joined the Navy and never came back.

R.C. returned to carpentry. Perhaps he was glad to get out of law enforcement and away from that boss and the enemies he had made on the job. One day soon after their marriage, he and Viva were in the Pep Cafe downtown having dinner. A man from San Augustine County had taken a pistol away from a constable and had a score to settle with R.C. Pace. When the man arrived at the cafe, he quickly learned what a mistake he had made. R.C. wasted no bullets. He took his own pistol and hit the man in the head with the barrel of the gun. This left a gash right down the middle of the man's forehead. Since the cafe stood across from the southwest corner of the courthouse, it was a short trip to deposit him in jail.

The couple made their first home in a sawmill camp in the north part of the county, where R.C. found work as a carpenter, building housing for the workers. His mother's boarding house burned to the ground early in 1923 as a result of poor wiring of the refrigerator (one of the town's first). Everyone escaped, but very little in the way of family belongings survived. She moved to a new house on East Houston Street, where the couple was living around the time of the birth of their first child, a daughter, in October of 1923.

In marrying Viva, R.C. demonstrated an appreciation for a strong-willed and practical woman who, in many ways, resembled his own mother. Safronia Frances Hall Pace by this time was around sixty, but still going strong. Her childhood had been spent in Thomasville, Georgia, during the Civil War and the years after. She was a mere toddler when her father went to war and she had never known him. He died a few years later in a prison camp in Columbus, Ohio. She and her brother Bill, her mother, Mary, and her grandfather suffered near-starvation on their small farm. Her determination is best reflected in a family legend.

Fannie and her brother were small and her grandfather, William Hancock, was crippled. They were a meager help to Mary Hancock Hall on the farm. Still, they grew a little corn and other vegetables. One morning, Mary rode a horse to the gristmill to grind the corn into meal. It was a dangerous mission and she told the children that she might not return. The river had been high and Mary swam the horse across it to the mill. She ground the corn and made cornbread when she returned.

Fannie took her piece of bread outside to eat. There was an old goose in the yard and it grabbed her bread and ate it. It made the girl so mad, she picked up the goose and wrung its neck. She then marched in the house and told her mother, "Mother, here's your damned old goose." In normal times, such crude talk was severely punished. In this instance, her mother just said, "Fannie, if I hadn't of known that you were so hungry, I would blister you for talking ugly, but I'll have to overlook you this time."

Fannie was always bitter about the deprivation the family endured in the war. Sixty years later, she was still telling her grandchildren, "The devil wore a blue uniform." She also took some pleasure from scaring them at night by saying that if they didn't go to sleep, the Yankees would get them!

After the war, the Halls sailed to Texas from Florida. They first landed in Galveston, and then from there, took a sailboat up the Sabine River, landing on Fannie's twelfth birthday in 1872. They camped in Newton County with relatives who had arrived earlier. The family soon settled in Jasper County in the tiny community of Peachtree. Fannie was always known for her fierce self-sufficiency. Her early deprivation led her to grow a large garden, including corn for grinding into meal. She made quilts and taught her daughter and granddaughters those skills, including the art of combing the seeds from homegrown cotton to use as batting.

With the arrival of her first granddaughter in 1923, Fannie was not shy when it came to showering the baby with attention, to the consternation of her new daughter-in-law. R.C. proved to be quite involved with the new baby himself. The daughter was named Aileen Frances. From the beginning, her father called her "Pete" or sometimes "Peter Frances." He often used nicknames and he gave no explanation for this one.

The infant cried a lot and R.C. joked that, "I never could tell what kind of face my daughter had because she was always crying!" One day, R.C. decided the baby was hungry and took some warm milk from his cow and fixed the baby a bottle. Raw cow's milk was not thought to be safe for a baby and Viva threw a fit, saying, "You're gonna kill her!" R.C. stood firm, though, and said, "Well, if I kill her, she'll die YOUNG. But she's gonna die FULL." Then he gave his baby some milk.

The baby went to sleep. It was the first night's rest the couple had enjoyed. Viva tried to blame Fannie for the baby's fussiness. The doting grandmother liked to sit and rock the infant all day in front of her sunny bay windows. Viva complained that this meant the baby was awake at night. R.C. was caught in the middle.

It was probably a wise decision for R.C. and Viva to quickly move to a rented house on the corner of Peachtree and West Houston Street. R.C. found work driving a soda water truck for Phil Scarborough. This took him all over the county and he got to know many people, black and white, in the tiny communities in the deep woods. He delivered soft drinks to small stores and to church revival meetings. There were occasional baseball games and people liked to go to the games and drink a "Big Red," the red soda water so popular in the South. Robert, his first son, was born in 1924, and he rode along with his father. Sometimes Fannie Pace's brother Bill, an old bachelor, accompanied them.

At that time, Jasper was small and life in town held few amenities. The house where the Pace family lived was lit by gas lamps. There was no electricity or indoor plumbing. Paved streets and numbered houses had not yet arrived. The Pace family's neighbors across the street kept goats. Watching the goats being milked was big entertainment for the children. Even with their usual chores, the children still found time for mischief. Once, they got the idea that Santa Claus could not find them because of the fire in the fireplace. Their solution was to take a hammer and knock a hole in the chimney. R.C. and Viva used the standard punishment of the time - a strong spanking.

Two more daughters were born in that rented house and by 1930, the family made a move to a new home on the Newton Highway. R.C. purchased the ten-acre property from a local businessman, David Henderson.

1930

★★★★★

Chapter Four

R.C., now thirty-nine, went back to work as a carpenter and began his biggest personal project: his own home. At the beginning of the Great Depression, the family moved into a two-room house on the property while construction proceeded. Life was a struggle for the growing family, and two more sons were born at the new place, for a total of six children. The sense of community that helped earlier generations of the family survive was strong in both R.C. and Viva. People shared when they could.

The Paces always had plenty of milk, keeping several cows at a time. They sometimes lent one out to the neighbors. During the height of the Depression, a child starved to death down the road. Perhaps pride kept that family from telling others how they were in desperate straits. It was a time when no one had money but many had food, since every family grew as big a garden as possible.

Jasper County life was not devastated by the Depression as severely as other places. The harsh reality remained that most everyone was equally poor before the Depression and stayed that way. Even the wealthiest business people in the area raised their own food and butchered their own animals. While today there are more defined social classes, back then the majority of people, black and white, struggled at a survival level.

There was a strong sense of community that kept people on top of that struggle. People shared when they butchered hogs or cattle. If there was a big crop of peas or other staples, it was shared with those who didn't have as much.

Mostly, that sense of community remained segregated, blacks helping blacks, whites helping whites. R.C. was one of the few whites who sometimes went out of his way to help blacks. He had to struggle to raise the food to support his large family, but still managed to take in a black couple which had nowhere to live. The couple, remembered only as Ada and Marcellus, lived several years in his barn and helped out around the house. Many of his children recall them as a part of the life on the Newton highway.

In 1936, R.C.'s sister, Beulah Eddy, ran for county treasurer and won. Her election continued a Pace tradition in Texas. From the arrival of the family in the 1820s, Pace family members had held county or district jobs. Besides their father, Hardy, who was a district clerk, Beulah and R.C.'s grandfather, Eli Pace, had been sheriff briefly in Jasper County. Their great-grandfather, also named Hardy, had served as a county commissioner in Jasper. He settled in Jasper on a land grant that had been given to his stepfather by Mexico.

Also in 1936, construction began on a new county jail, and R.C. found his skills put to use in building it. Beaver Bishop had been voted out of office in favor of A.G. Maxwell in 1928, but Beaver continued to run every two years, trying to get back into office. By 1938, Maxwell thought he had settled into a steady position as sheriff. It all came unraveled one day.

A local young man, Wilton Smith, came to town early to open up at a gas station where he worked. He passed by a men's clothing store downtown and was surprised to find the door open. He went in to investigate and found Paul Maxwell, the sheriff's son, and a few other boys. Young Maxwell claimed to have walked in on a robbery. He said he had tried to call the store's owner but got no answer, despite the early hour of the call. Wilton grabbed the phone and tried again. He gave his request to the operator - this was in the day when, instead of a dial tone, the operator asked, "Number, please." The owner answered on the first ring. It was soon apparent that Maxwell and his friends were the burglars. Boldly, they had stored stolen loot in the clock tower of the courthouse itself. R.C. was amused by the crime, and by the fact that the sheriff was oblivious to his son's sudden wealth. "If it were me and mine," he said, borrowing a legal phrase, "if they come in with something I don't know about, I'll serve notice to show cause where it comes from!"

In 1937, Fannie Pace, whose health had been failing, passed away. Her funeral was one of the few instances where people saw R.C. cry in public. That loss may have caused him to re-evaluate his life, because he decided to run for sheriff. With Maxwell discredited, Beaver Bishop stood a chance of coming back. Many people held strong, unfavorable opinions of Beaver Bishop.

On the other hand, Pace had built a solid reputation. His brief job on the soda water truck helped him to be well known all over the county. As a carpenter, he was respected and known as an honest and hard worker. Those traits were generally enough to qualify to run for the office of sheriff at that time.

A three-way race ensued, with Beaver Bishop getting many votes, but Pace and Maxwell ended up in a run-off. The final vote was Pace with 1398 votes, and 1212 for Maxwell. Maxwell had served since 1929. R.C., now 47, began a new life as an elected official.

Chapter Five

R.C. Pace had run for sheriff on a platform of fair and equal treatment, with no favoritism. This was not always the way with sheriffs in Jasper County, or for that matter, the citizens of the county. There were numerous, longstanding relationships that developed in the small towns and settlements. People emigrated from the same town in Georgia or Tennessee to one settlement, and then intermarried among themselves for several generations. This gave rise to a closeness that was supportive, but also isolating. A sheriff had to serve the whole county, which was not an easy task if people in the north part of the county were suspicious of those in the south part. Many sheriffs in Jasper's history were known for going easy on friends in their area. This had turned people against Beaver Bishop, as well as A.G. Maxwell.

For the black citizens of the county, segregation was the ongoing favoritism that worked against their lives. In the late 30s, a black person was required to move off a sidewalk if a white person passed. To shop in local businesses, blacks waited for any and all whites to be served first. The wait could be an hour or longer. Local shopkeepers would serve them any day of the week which was not true across the state. In Corpus Christi during that decade, for example, blacks were only permitted to shop on Saturday mornings. In addition, church services there were monitored and if they grew too boisterous by local standards, the police ordered churchgoers out of their own worship services. There is no evidence this happened in Jasper.

Buying on credit was another area of discrimination. In an area where most people lived from paycheck to paycheck or from one harvest to the next, the ability to borrow money was essential. One local businessman found himself a profitable, but unscrupulous, enterprise as a loan shark. Sheriff Pace received many complaints from the black community about the extreme interest rates this man charged them. No doubt, many of the borrowers overpaid their small loans - often as little as $5 - many times over. The sheriff moved quickly to put a halt to the business, telling people to pay off the loans but forget the interest. Besides being fair, this was a shrewd political move. He quickly gained support of many black citizens whose votes he needed. He also built trust. Key to any law enforcement in a rural community is information. A sheriff who inspired only fear was not one people sought out to give details of a crime. This foundation of trust was the essential element of Sheriff Pace's success.

Ready to handle any serious crimes that came his way in January 1939, R.C. first had to handle a crime of a burglar with a sweet tooth! The Jasper Bake Shop had experienced several burglaries by a thief who took cash and cake. This was an easy case to solve, but by spring there was a murder in town. In the midst of a domestic argument, a local woman attacked her husband with a knife and he shot her. Other crimes that year were bank robberies and burglaries and hog theft.

Most of the crimes could be handled with little assistance, and had to be. Sheriff Pace was essentially alone in his job. There was a night watchman, and some recall a few deputies. Still, when the sheriff was called out at night, he made his own posse. One situation in particular called for this.

Up at the northwestern edge of Jasper County there is a small settlement called Blue Hole. Its name is derived from an old quarry filled with blue water. The people who lived there (mostly black) had become frightened of a local black man. The man was known to get drunk and tear up local stores, and generally create mayhem. He was no favorite to the white community, either. He lived with a white woman - a scandal in that day, and illegal in many states. Sheriff Pace tried to arrest the man several times. The man was cunning and hid out in the woods for long periods.

Since the man was known to be violent, Sheriff Pace called a few of his trusted friends to assist him. Different men went out on several attempts to arrest the man. Among them were "Uncle" Jim Hicks and Ray Baldwin, both local businessmen who hunted with him. Baldwin had been in the military police in World War I, so he had a bit of skill in law enforcement. The men learned that the wanted man would be in his girlfriend's house, and went there at night and surrounded it. Stories vary here about what happened. The man refused to come out peacefully - either ran or tried to grab a gun - and was shot and killed.

A shocking discovery followed the death. The man's girlfriend had given birth to several infants, whose bodies were found under the porch of the house. Some claimed they were stillborn, but many believed they had been murdered. With the man dead, the girlfriend, who was from another state, left town in a hurry. No further investigation occurred.

Because the man was killed during an arrest, the sheriff took full responsibility for the action. Once his body was brought to town to the funeral home, Sheriff Pace went home to tell his family. The sheriff warned his six children that they would hear that when their father had tried to make an arrest, a man had been killed. He told them it was a sad situation, but part of his job as sheriff. Unlike previous times when black people were killed locally by law enforcement without apology, this event brought no celebration. Still, it was quite memorable, and numerous people claim to have seen the body in the funeral home, including the sheriff's oldest daughter. People spoke in whispers about it for some time. Interestingly, there is strong reason to believe that it was not Sheriff Pace who killed the man. Two people who viewed the body recognized a familiar bullet pattern from another man's gun. The incident was never mentioned in the local newspaper.

As R.C. settled into his role as sheriff, his family life became an extension of his work. Viva was paid a small fee to prepare the daily meals for prisoners. The family garden - always big enough to feed a large family - was expanded. It was a common sight to see prisoners who were working off their fines doing labor in the garden or around the house. The children did their chores side by side with bootleggers and other rough characters, which they came to know by name. These prisoners ("birds" or "jailbirds" to the kids) drove the children to school, cooked, cleaned, tended livestock, and babysat through the years.

It was as part of this merging of family and work life that the sheriff called on his sons to help him. Because he rarely had deputies - especially in the middle of the night - he took his oldest son, Robert, along. Sheriff Pace was not alone in recruiting the boys for county business. Once a judge sent Robert to the Huntsville prison to pick up an inmate who had a court hearing back in Jasper. At that time, the drive to Huntsville was a difficult one, requiring a trip by ferry across the Neches River. When the boy - all of about 15 - arrived at the prison, the warden at first refused to turn the prisoner over to "a kid." The boy insisted that he could not return to Jasper without the prisoner and the warden relented. They made the trip home safely. The prisoner no doubt was nervous about a teenage boy with a pistol!

There were times when the sheriff had to go alone. One day in May 1940, the elderly bailiff, Mr. Wheatley, was taking a prisoner from the jail to a hearing next door in the courthouse. The prisoner, E. J. McLane, had made a career of burglarizing small businesses. Perhaps knowing that he was heading to the penitentiary, McLane overpowered the old bailiff and made a run for it. He stole a car parked nearby and fled.

Sheriff Pace was always shorthanded, but even more so on this day. Word had just come down of a bank robbery south of Jasper in Kirbyville. Every available man was in hot pursuit of the pair of robbers. The two fled to the Neches River, where one drowned and the other was captured. Their plan was to hide out in the dense forest known as the Big Thicket. It was a popular one for criminals. The pair had camping gear with them when they went in the river, and that was recovered. The money ($2655) was never found.

Meanwhile, back in Jasper, E. J. McLane was on the run. He picked up his wife and they headed north, eventually abandoning the car in the woods. Sheriff Pace was determined to bring him back. He followed the man on horseback, taking a bloodhound named Old Henry to follow the scent. R.C. was relentless. He trailed McLane through the night into dense woods. Scratched and with torn clothes, he kept on. At one point, the fugitive couple - fearful of the hound - ran into the home of a black couple and tried to hide in their bed! McLane's wife stayed there and he kept going. Sheriff Pace outlasted him. He tied McLane with ropes and brought him back toward town the next day. They stopped for water on the way at a small store. While R.C. caught his breath, the prisoner managed to get himself untied and made one more run across a field. R.C. mustered his last bit of strength and tackled the man to the ground. Now, R.C. was mad. He tied a rope around E.J. and forced him to walk the several miles back to town while he rode behind him on his horse.

They were quite a sight, coming down Main Street. R.C. had lost his glasses as well as his false teeth (which he rarely wore, but kept handy in his pocket). His clothes, sturdy khaki, were in shreds.

R.C.'s relentless nature served him well, again and again. His family marveled at his ability to shut out everything to work a case. "Dogged" is the word repeatedly used. He had a favorite saying, using the analogy of the hunter who used hounds: "If we strike this trail and can get to where we can bark, let's don't quit 'til we get a man treed." The pressure of a case seemed to push him to another level of focus and high energy.

The letdown after a case was not as easy for R.C., or his family. When he had time off, he frequently drank. Sometimes he would drink for several days. Never violent, but deeply inebriated, his behavior infuriated his wife. Viva enjoyed the prestige of being the sheriff's wife. She was an intelligent woman who had tremendous enthusiasm for civic activities. She ran her home with the energy and the creativity of a person who did not have much in life. She was a scrapper, like R.C., making good use of what little they had. Still, there was nothing she could do about the drinking. At one point, she refused to let him drink in the house, so he hid a bottle in the barn. One day, he went out back to drink and was unable find the bottle. One of the boys found it and said, "Daddy, is this what you are looking for?" After that incident, he stopped hiding the bottle in the barn and found other places to drink.

Usually he would "go off on a toot" for a few days then go for weeks or even months with the drinking under control. He managed to be efficient in the job and Jasper seemed content to have him in office. The popular saying was that "R.C. Pace was a better sheriff drunk than most men were sober." He won his next election easily.

1941

★ ★ ★ ★ ★

Chapter Six

The outside world encroached on the quiet rural life as young men were drafted for the war effort. R.C. remembered the horrors he had seen in World War I and hated it when Robert, his oldest boy, got his notice. He even tried to persuade the draft board to take him - a 50-year-old man - in the boy's place. Robert went into the Army and was sent to the Philippines. Ailene, R.C.'s oldest daughter, married and stayed nearby when her husband was sent to the Aleutian Islands off the coast of Alaska.

With so many men away and bullets in short supply, these were relatively calm years for law enforcement. In 1940, fighting broke out in downtown Jasper between Jehovah's Witnesses and local citizens, but that was settled when the town passed an "anti-leafleting" ordinance. Still, there was a shortage of men for the sheriff to call on. The next son in the family was enlisted to help.

One difficulty for a small town in wartime was the lack of a medical examiner. If there was a need for an autopsy, Pace had to send his son to Austin - eight hours round trip - driving fast with the body. One memorable day, his son, Hardy (about 15 years old at the time), drove one body to Austin, returned, then had to take another body right back.

Going out on arrests with the sheriff could be a highly stressful experience. There was no telling what might happen, but armed with a shotgun, the young man was ready.

Once a man got in a fight with several friends, shooting them with number six squirrel shot. He was a man R.C. knew well. When he was repeatedly arrested for various crimes, R. C. had a talk with him. It was a talk he gave to many criminals who visited his jail too many times. He told the man, "This county is not big enough for you and me, and I have family here and can't leave. You have to go because I don't want to see you no more." This speech was called "putting the sun on him." The man left the county for a while, but returned. Sheriff Pace knew where to find the fellow and took his son along. He settled the boy in the trees behind the house and had him fill his gun with squirrel shot. He knew the man would run out the back door as soon as he saw the sheriff. Pace wanted him to receive a dose of his own medicine.

Sure enough, when Sheriff Pace knocked at the door, the man took off out the back door. When he saw the armed teenager, he stopped in midstep - his leg bent like a bird dog pointing - and exclaimed, "Why hellloooo Mister Hardy! I didn't know you were there!" R.C. and the boy burst out laughing, and hauled the man to jail.

Other arrests were less comical. Sheriff Pace enjoyed a reputation for treating women, black and white, with respect. A man who beat his wife could expect severe treatment. He used his blackjack on many a wife-beater. Sometimes he would position his son outside a house with a gun, go in the back way, and kick a man repeatedly out the front door, across the porch, and down the steps to his car. Pace had been raised to be polite and respectful to women, but the rare woman who crossed him felt his fire. He believed women deserved respect, but that they also needed to behave like ladies. In one sad case, he took one of his sons to arrest a couple who were neglecting their infant child. He entered the house to find the man and wife both drunk and the child filthy and hungry. He kicked the man out the door in his usual style. Then the sheriff grabbed the woman by her hair and yelled, "You are gonna get up and take care of that child or I am gonna throw you in jail and take the kid to the orphans' home!"

Sometimes there was little that Sheriff Pace could do when family life fell apart. In March 1941, E.D. McClannahan had marital problems and his wife returned to her parents. Her father, W.W. Carruth, even went to the sheriff to discuss his concern. Mrs. McClannahan filed for divorce. Her husband was enraged and went to the Carruth home, grabbed his wife, and took her back to his home. When her father went to check on her safety, four shots were fired. Carruth was killed. E.D. was charged with murder. Two months later, he was tried, convicted, and sentenced to twenty years for murder.

Fortunately, murder was not a regular occurrence in town. Some weeks, there were no serious crimes reported in the newspaper at all. Most of the paper was now filled with stories of the war effort. But one crime that never slowed down was burglary. Burglary rings enjoyed a long and colorful history in Jasper County. Way back in 1901, unknown persons blew up a safe in a downtown burglary attempt. The resultant fire burned almost the entire downtown. Jewelry stores and wholesale grocers were favorite targets.

The Santa Fe Railroad Depot became the site of numerous burglaries in 1941. A gang selected it for ease, since there was little to steal. On June 12th, a mere twenty-five dollars was taken when the door was broken. While the outer door was sent away for repairs in July, thieves broke in and grabbed of a case of snuff.

Sheriff Pace was not ignoring these burglaries. He investigated leads all over the county. In late July, the local newspaper reported that the sheriff was tracking down a man in connection with the burglaries on old State Highway 8 (12 miles north of Jasper) when his car ran into a ditch. Badly bruised but otherwise unharmed, the sheriff continued to investigate.

The case was broken later in the year when an employee of a jewelry store surprised one of the burglars, who ran to a nearby house and was captured. A man and woman were arrested. Somehow, the leader of the ring escaped. In the house where the two were caught, the sheriff recovered jewelry, watches and even the case of snuff.

In some ways, the town was more endangered by illness and accidents - the same threats faced by the pioneers who first settled there. That summer in 1941, there were eleven cases of malaria in the county. Malaria cases typically rise when there are periods of heavy rain, allowing more mosquitoes than usual to breed. Rats were also a problem. The newspaper proudly reported that a rodent campaign resulted in hundreds of rats killed in the downtown area. The advent of effective antibiotics and vaccines brought new health clinics to the area. Local ministers gave approval to health classes explaining venereal diseases to the public. It was not too soon - by October, over ten thousand visits were recorded by Jasper and Newton County venereal disease clinics.

The relative quiet brought on by the war gave R.C. a bit more time to enjoy his favorite relaxation - hunting. He had always been an avid hunter - a necessity for the poor farmer's son and now a family man with a house full of children. Along with his friends Ray Baldwin, Uncle Jim Hicks, and others, he set up camp in the woods and the men hunted deer with hounds. In the fall of that year, a fox and wolf hunt was organized that brought thousands of hunters from all over the state.

These outings were a time when the sheriff could find relief from the pressures of his work. He saw the dark side of life in the county and it made him cynical. With these friends, he could hunt and eat and laugh. Baldwin was a quiet man who did not drink, but he had a penetrating wit. Uncle Jim Hicks loved to talk and drink. Sometimes the men would take along a black man to cook for them (possibly a prisoner). Late at night after considerable drinking, R.C. and the cook would sing Negro spirituals. Sometimes the men would bring along their sons. The boys were given all the difficult work - moving and skinning deer, or whatever was needed. Their hard work was not rewarded, for they were teased without mercy if the men were inclined. Once, R.C.'s son Hardy was sitting on a log trying to sleep off a hangover. A young deer jumped out of the woods and over the log. The boy shot a few times halfheartedly but missed. After that incident, and for years to come, Baldwin teased the boy. Hardy could never deride anyone else for a mistake in Baldwin's presence, because the old man would stop him cold by saying, "Now, HOW close was that deer when you shot at it?"

On another occasion, R.C. lent a dog to some friends for a hunt. After a few days, the dog returned home, a straggly mess and very jumpy. Pace tracked the men to their camp and interrogated them. "What did you do? My dog came home and BIT me!" The men had been doing more drinking than hunting, and in their excitement, had shot off their guns in all directions, scaring the dog. Once again, R.C. and his friends used the incident for teasing the men for long afterward.

These relaxed moments were a welcome relief for the sheriff. Pace loved to be outdoors sitting around a campfire with his friends. He had meat or fish cooked in a way that was less well done than others might prefer, so he could eat without his false teeth. One night he was sitting with friends and they all began to complain about how they could not eat corn with their false teeth, or enjoy a steak with their false teeth. Sheriff Pace just laughed and said, "I can't THINK with my false teeth!"

Occasionally, the sheriff found pleasurable moments on the job. One night he had a call that a soldier was drunk and stumbling around on the highway. The sheriff took him to jail to sleep it off. The next day the young soldier explained to the sheriff how friends had brought him to town. Once the young man was drunk, his friends had left him on the road with his gun. The young man was quite worried that the sheriff would report him, because being found in that condition with his weapon was a serious offense. Sheriff Pace must have felt some sympathy for him, because he had never been in Jasper before. Instead of giving him a fine, R.C. just looked at the young soldier and began to remark how it was so hard to do any hunting with bullets in short supply. The more he talked, the more he looked at the soldier's ammunition. After a few minutes of this exchange, the grateful soldier gave him four boxes of ammunition and was sent on his way.

Also during the war, a house of prostitution began operating in downtown Jasper. Jasper was a 'dry' county, meaning that liquor was not sold there legally. The madam of the brothel had a different plan and the house served liquor along with the ladies. Because of that, a liquor control board operation began that brought in undercover men to visit the house and then make arrests for serving alcohol. The female owner of the establishment called Pace when the arrests were made and complained loudly that one of these officers had insulted her. As always, Pace gave women respect, provided they behaved like ladies. This time, he noted her chosen profession and said wryly, "Now, just HOW in the HELL did he do that?"

By the end of 1941, Pace had succeeded in getting highway patrol officers on the county roads. This was long overdue - car accidents were all too frequent. There was a Christmas murder of a woman in Evadale - her husband and two others were charged.

Pace had now been in office for two terms, and as the 1942 primaries approached, he was quite secure in the job. One opponent withdrew from the race in April, and Pace ran unopposed in the Democratic primary in July. As Jasper was a one-party county, he was set for two more years.

1943

★ ★ ★ ★ ★

Chapter Seven

As the war continued, Jasper became a staging area for troop maneuvers. The sudden appearance of hundreds of soldiers created a variety of problems. Once, soldiers on leave bought out the food and supplies in the whole town - not a piece of bread was left for the locals. In some towns in the South, riots had broken out as black soldiers from outside the South chafed at the strict segregation that was in place. This did not happen in Jasper, but it was always a concern.

Sheriff Pace had a more personal concern at this time. He had two attractive teenage daughters who he wanted to keep under his protective eye. His sons were drawn into his work and exposed to the dangerous situations that the sheriff himself faced. Pace was quite the protector, though, when it came to his girls. When the soldiers were in town, he told his daughters to stay at home. Still, he could not monitor every moment of their free time.

All the children had outside jobs as soon as they were old enough. In fact, from the time they could walk, they were expected to do chores. The smallest pulled weeds in the garden. The boys milked the cows and when the cows were herded, the boys chased the cows out of thick bushes, acting as "cowdogs." Sometimes the boys were given a calf to raise and sell. In those days, their families gave children serious responsibilities, so in this way Pace was not harsher than anyone else. For example, Pace knew a black farmer who made excellent tool handles and other farm implements. He had bought things from the farmer for years and knew his children. The farmer's oldest boy, whom Pace called "Little Buck," worked at chores similar to Pace's own boys. When the farmer became ill, though, this child was forced to quit school at age thirteen to support his family. Jasper had few jobs for such a young boy, so he hitched to Corpus Christi (a day's drive) and worked for two years, shoveling seashells into a truck. The shells were used in highway construction. Living in a rented room and eating crackers and canned meat, Little Buck earned enough to provide for his family until his father recovered. Despite the harshness, it was not an unusual situation. This was the tradition of the county - all family members contributed to the family survival.

This rural way of life may explain how Pace was able to demand so much from his sons. He often put them, if not exactly in harm's way, at least in some very unsafe situations. He demanded that they show something of his own fearlessness, counseling one boy, "Be humble and don't stumble."

As much as he included the boys in his often-gloomy work, he sought to shield his daughters from those dangers he knew only too well. Jasper was a dry county, and as such, was generally free of wild dance halls, but the surrounding counties were not. Young people who were not involved in the war effort frequented these places, where brawls were commonplace.

Typical of these clubs was one run by Frank Arnold in Silsbee, a town south of Jasper. Arnold was quite a character, running a hall that featured barbecue and live music. He ran ads on the local radio station that went something like this:

Bring your brass knuckles
And the other fellow's wife
And come to Frank Arnold's
For the time of your life!

Arnold served food and drink to both black and white people in his place - he said, "I don't give a damn what color a man is, as long as he has money!"

His path did not generally cross the sheriff's since his business was in another county. Arnold owned a farm in Jasper, however, which brought him there regularly. At the time, Sheriff Pace's daughter, Mary, worked at the local AAA (Agricultural Adjustment Administration) office. The AAA was an agricultural agency begun in the New Deal days to support farm prices, which had dropped by 50% in the first few years of the Great Depression. Frank Arnold came in often and Mary was always polite, which was not the reaction he got from everyone. Arnold had a brusque manner and sense of humor - as shown by his radio ads - that offended many people. Mary was also a beauty with dark hair and eyes and no doubt she charmed the man. Frank was in the office one day near Christmas and sought to thank her for her kindness. He asked her if she liked beer, and she admitted that she enjoyed a glass occasionally. A few days later, a case of beer was delivered to her - at the sheriff's office!

When Mary came home from work following the delivery, R.C. and Viva were waiting for her. They stood side by side at the door, a sure sign that this was a grave matter. Her father demanded to know just how she was acquainted with a notorious fellow like Frank Arnold. When she explained how he came in the AAA office and had offered her the beer, R.C. relaxed. His daughter's reputation was safe, so he allowed himself to enjoy the unexpected gift.

It was easy enough for Sheriff Pace to accept the gift from Frank Arnold, as the man had no dealings in Jasper that might require the sheriff's scrutiny. Others who tried to bribe him lived to regret it. Their lives were made that much harder. R.C. had the strength of character to resist bribery, although his salary was meager, and only supplemented by the fines he received. As much as he was honest, Pace simply was not a greedy man. He had always lived a frugal life. He took pride in being self-sufficient, a lesson he learned most strongly from his mother. He lacked expensive habits; he played dominoes, but was no gambler. He kept no girlfriends, and drinking was a cheap vice. His idea of entertainment was to organize his friends into the "Five C" organization. The men met at the Pep Hotel (owned by his friend Ray Baldwin) for an old fashioned dinner of "coon, collards, chitterlings, cracklin' bread and coffee."

As 1943 dragged on, there was a surprising twist to an old case. Roy Greer, the escaped ringleader of the Santa Fe burglary gang, turned up in Yakima, Washington. Arrangements were made for Sheriff Pace and a sheriff from Sabine County to drive out to California, where the prisoner would be waiting. It was a hard trip in a non-air-conditioned car. While they were away, two black boys, ages ten and twelve, were sent to the reformatory for murder - they cut the throat of a 13-year-old friend. Their father brought them to the court, where they pled guilty to the charges. The newspaper reported few details.

The two sheriffs left on July 16, 1943, but a week later, Viva reported to the newspaper that the sheriff from Sabine County had taken ill. In reality, the other sheriff had an emotional breakdown of some kind in California. R.C. was forced to return with the prisoner alone. He drove at night all the way back, trying to escape the intense July heat in the desert. When he arrived in Abilene, he had Greer locked up in jail for the night so he could finally sleep. The men returned safely home and the prisoner went back to jail for his crimes.

By 1945, crime was back on the increase. Some convicts from a prison farm escaped and blew through town. They took a game warden hostage, stopped for gas, and had a quick meal at the Chat 'N Chew Cafe before leaving Sheriff Pace's jurisdiction. The manufacturing of moonshine continued to be a popular career choice in the impoverished county. The newspapers reported early that year that 45 stills had been found and destroyed. There were several killings that resulted from drunken fights. One man, Tiny Fisher, was arrested for keeping a gambling house. Tiny was a regular "bird" out at the Pace home, always in trouble for fighting or other activities.

The round-the-clock nature of crime strained the Pace's family life. Family outings were subject to cancellation at any moment. In the late 1930s, when the family first moved to the Newton Highway property, the whole neighborhood gathered at the Pace home every Fourth of July for a picnic. A barbecued goat was often the main course. On other occasions, Pace took the whole family out to Aldridge, in the northwest part of the county, where his uncle, John Pace, had a small farm. The farm had been home to Pace's grandfather, Eli Pace, for a time, when he ran a ferry across the Neches River. On the property was a simple wood farmhouse with a long porch across the front. When electricity came to the rural area, the men of the house used their pistols to shoot holes in the walls to run through the electrical wires. Pace's children and their Pace cousins sometimes camped out near the river for a few days. The children found turtle eggs on sandbars along the river.

These family campouts became difficult when Pace took on the sheriff's job. One year on the Fourth, the sheriff made plans to take the family to a rodeo. In the morning, he went in to work, where three prisoners were serving their time. Viva set to work on the noon meal for the three. When Pace returned to pick up the meal, the plan had changed. He now had forty prisoners - for offenses ranging from fights to drunkenness. Viva and the girls had to work until 3 p.m. to cook enough food for the inmates. The rodeo was soon forgotten.

One afternoon in April 1945, Pace received a call. A local man, Zeke Bradshaw, had gone to the bus station and shot Mrs. Bennie Booker with a .38 pistol. This was rumored to be a romance gone sour and Zeke attempted to stop the woman from leaving town. Mrs. Booker, who had two of her seven children with her, was only wounded, and people in the bus station bravely wrestled the pistol away from Bradshaw. Sheriff Pace took Hardy along to find Zeke. At the Bradshaw home a short while later, Mrs. Bradshaw came running down the road, saying that Zeke had taken a shotgun and gone into the woods. Sheriff Pace and Hardy tried in vain to find him. Hardy was terrified. He knew that if they came upon Bradshaw, his target would be the sheriff. This was a heavy responsibility for a teenage boy. They trailed the man through the night in the woods, but with no luck.

In the early morning, the men were in front of the house when Bradshaw emerged from the woods clutching his chest. As he drew closer, he pulled back his hands to reveal that he had turned his gun on himself. His shoulder blade was pulled back to reveal his beating heart. The Bradshaws had no telephone to call an ambulance, so Hardy drove to town to get one. Zeke Bradshaw died the next day.

Around the same time, a man scuffled with a city marshal down in Kirbyville. He shot and wounded the marshal and escaped. Again, Pace and Hardy searched the roads for him. They had no success, but the next day the man was shot and killed by deputies in Newton County. Sheriff Pace picked up the body and brought it to Jasper in his car trunk. The Kirbyville marshal arrived later to view the criminal's body. He was so angry about the attack that he took aim and emptied his pistol into the corpse - leaving bullet holes in Pace's 1940 Mercury.

In the summer of 1945, a trial was moved from Orange County to Jasper. The defendant, Dr. Carpenter, was a professional gambler charged with gambling activity in the city of Orange. Carpenter was a diabetic and needed regular meals. Sheriff Pace brought him out to his house for lunch during the court recess. Carpenter was a flashy and talkative fellow. He entertained the family with tales of his gambling exploits. Once, while in Mexico, the man bragged, he won "a bushel basket full of money." He complained loudly that when he changed the money at the border, "It wasn't but ten thousand dollars!"

Carpenter was found guilty of all charges, a verdict that enraged his high-strung Cajun wife. She took her walking stick and began to beat the jurors! A week later, the newspaper reported that she was fined $100 and given three days in jail for attacking the jury.

When 1946 arrived, Pace readied himself for another election. There was more competition now and the sheriff had to campaign hard. His drinking was always an issue. Other candidates were emphatic when they described themselves as "sober" in campaign advertisements. The regular campaigning (with elections every two years) had made Pace a savvy politician and he used his wit to deflate opponents. Once he gave a speech in which he declared, "It has been rumored that I drink enough whiskey to float this courthouse. That's a lie. But there might be enough to walk knee-deep in it!"

The early part of the year was busy for crime as well - two murder/suicides in April, reckless bus drivers, and something new on the scene: complaints of a wave of juvenile delinquency. Around this time, a boy of about six years of age was found walking alone on a country road. Locals called the sheriff, who discovered the child's parents had left town without him. There were no social services for this situation, so Pace took the boy home. He and Viva took care of the child for a few weeks until R.C. located his parents in a nearby county. The parents had surely never heard anything like the anger the sheriff reserved for them. The idea of anyone neglecting a child was unthinkable to him. No doubt the threats he made to the pair were convincing. No one wanted to incur the wrath of Sheriff Pace. As tough as he could be, he had a warm and nurturing side. Returning to Jasper after delivering the boy to his parents, he was unusually quiet and thoughtful.

By the time the primary rolled around in August, many of the contenders had dropped out of the race and Pace found himself running against a surprising opponent: Beaver Bishop. Now sixty years old, and with a new wife (Mae Stephenson had passed away), old Beaver just had to make one more try at the sheriff's job. He still had considerable support, and in the August 1st primary, he led Pace by sixteen votes, forcing a run-off. This was a wake-up call for Pace's supporters and they got out the vote. A few weeks later, Pace defeated Bishop, receiving 2072 votes to Bishop's 1548.

Two months later, Beaver went deer hunting with his friend, attorney Glen Faver. Somehow Faver mistook the six foot seven Bishop for a deer, and shot and killed him. Hunting accidents were not unusual in the county and the papers reported several down through the years. The mix of adrenaline and alcohol caused many a hunter to misjudge his target. Beaver Bishop also had a habit of wearing a tan colored jacket and that color in the woods could appear similar to a deer.

Still, this time popular opinion was against Glen Faver. From Viva Pace and through the town, almost everyone suspected it was intentional. It was the subject of intense gossip, and folks said, "The boys at the barber shop never did think it was anything but murder." The locals clearly had a low opinion of Glen Faver and believed he could have done it. Perhaps just as strongly, many people could only think of Beaver dying at the hands of an enemy - he had gained so many over his life. Beaver had served as sheriff from 1918 to 1928. Some thought that perhaps Beaver Bishop "had it coming," but fifty years later it is still argued. No charges were ever filed. Beaver was buried locally. When his widow moved away, she had the casket exhumed and re-buried in Longview, Texas.

1947

★ ★ ★ ★ ★

Chapter Eight

The local whispers over Beaver Bishop had barely settled down by the following February when Josephine Elveston came to town one Saturday. Mrs. Elveston and her husband Alfred lived in Call, a tiny community seventeen miles from Jasper. She came from a prominent Newton family, the Grays, and this was her second marriage. She was fifty-two years old, fair and rotund, with long gray hair. Alfred Elveston worked at the Kirby Lumber Company, but had decided at the age of sixty to retire. This meant he would lose the $2000 group life insurance policy he held with the company, which did not agree with Josephine's plans. He planned a quiet retirement on their farm, supported by his Social Security payments, but his wife worried that he was going to leave her penniless. On the February 13th visit to Jasper, she went to an insurance agency and took out a $1000 policy on her husband. It became effective on February 18th.

On February 20th, Mrs. Elveston took some strychnine she had bought to kill insects. She filled a capsule with the poison. It was not very much poison, though, so she did not give it to her husband right away. She waited until February 24th, when she and Alfred went shopping again in Jasper. This time, she went to the Henderson Drug Store and purchased one-eighth ounce of strychnine. She hid the purchase in her purse.

A few days later, Josie found her opportunity. She had a daughter from her first marriage, Jeanette Herrin, who lived with the couple. Josie waited one morning for the girl to leave for school. Alfred had been feeling poorly and asked for some quinine capsules, which they kept on hand. She gave him the strychnine capsule instead. Alfred went outside for some air but quickly returned. With shocking intuition, he yelled, "You must have given me strychnine!"

Those were the only words he was able to say before convulsions took over. Josie sought help from a neighbor, but by the time a doctor arrived on the scene an hour later, Alfred Elveston was dead.

A funeral was planned immediately and family began to arrive. Alfred had a daughter from a previous marriage, Mrs. Alton Hale. She had quite a bit to say about Josephine Elveston, and went to speak to law officers at once. According to Mrs. Hale, Josie was suspiciously connected to the death of her first husband, Juan Herrin, as well as that of a fifteen year-old boy. Based on this new information, the local Justice of the Peace ordered an autopsy.

The funeral was about to begin when officers arrived to take the body for an autopsy. Vital organs were removed from Mr. Elveston's corpse and Sheriff Pace left at once for Austin, where there was a laboratory equipped to handle such cases. A few weeks later, the sheriff received the autopsy report, which confirmed death by poisoning.

R.C. brought in two Texas Rangers to help him with the case. Roscoe D. Holliday was a dapper man who was fifty-nine years old and a former sheriff himself. Only 5' 8" with blue eyes and gray hair, he made a strong show of authority when needed. He and Pace had developed a close working relationship. Often late at night, Ranger Holliday drove over to the Pace home. The children recognized the sound of his car, as he came out to the side porch to wait for the sheriff to get up from bed. There, the two men drank coffee - Pace took his with cream and no sugar - and discussed cases with each other. The two men were so skilled at capturing criminals that one local man commented that if he ever decided to commit a crime, first he would kill Pace and Holliday - because if he didn't, they surely would catch him!

Holliday was serious about his work and was quick to speak his mind. Once an FBI man came to town to ask questions and told Holliday that he wanted the Ranger to give a statement. "Listen, G-man," Holliday replied, "I don't give statements; I TAKE statements!" R.D. could be a practical joker, too. A favorite trick of his was putting a lipstick-stained cigarette in the ashtray or back floorboard of a married man's car. He even slipped condoms into a man's jacket pocket - creating havoc when the man's wife found it later! His humor could take a dark turn, understandable among law enforcement officers who deal with death on such a regular basis. Once he left some human remains from an autopsy in Pace's car, leaving the odor of human flesh for weeks.

Dick Middleton, on the other hand, was quiet and no-nonsense. Like Ranger Holliday, he had a strong presence and could take control of any unruly crowd. He once stood guard outside a courtroom in another county while a murder trial was in progress. It was a crime of passion, and family members of both defendant and victim became quite hostile outside the building. When he stepped up to take control of the situation, he transformed the group from an angry mob to a group more like a church congregation completely quiet and thoughtful! Middleton was a former sheriff from Center, a town north of Jasper. Younger than the other two, at forty-six he brought the similar experience of a county sheriff to the job.

The three men arrested Mrs. Elveston at home. She was cooking dinner and briefly wiped away a few tears on her apron when they arrived. That was the last visible emotion she revealed.

Sheriff Pace had his own methods for an interrogation. He removed all the chairs from his office and put in an old keg - some called it a pickle barrel - that the suspect used for a chair. Mrs. Elveston was a rather large lady and after a few hours on the keg, she must have been quite uncomfortable. When she began to talk, the picture of a serial killer emerged. She confessed to killing not only Alfred Elveston, but her previous husband, whose death had been described as "acute indigestion", and the son of a former employer, as well. She was what is now described as a "Black widow" serial killer, which is a woman who kills those close to her, often for personal gain. Research shows that a woman who kills in this way may commit ten or more murders before she is caught.

Indeed, people had been suspicious of Josie Elveston before, but nothing came of it. Her first husband, Juan Herrin, died suddenly in 1937. She had married the man when she was only sixteen, in 1911, so they were reasonably happy for over 25 years before she decided to kill him. If, as she confessed, this was her first murder, it still meant that she had a ten-year span during which she murdered three men. At this point in her life, she was older and more worried about money, so there is no way to know whom she might have targeted next.

Her second victim, H.E. Simmons, died in 1944, while Josie was working as a housekeeper for his father. Perhaps she thought the elder Mr. Simmons was a good prospect for marriage but that the boy interfered with her plans. This is only speculation, but typical of the motives of this type of serial killer. In fact, the boy's death was strange enough that an autopsy was done, and revealed poison. There was not enough evidence to bring charges, however, and the matter was dropped. It seems that she was caught in this last case because she was in a hurry. With her husband retiring at once, she had little time to plan and carry out the killing. It may have been that with her first husband she poisoned him slowly over a longer period of time. In this way, there would be no suspicion on her, his loyal wife of so many years.

Sheriff Pace was relieved to get a signed confession, but he continued to investigate. He was extremely thorough in every investigation, and he wanted no mistakes. He brought to his work an attention to detail from his years as a carpenter. This was a man who drew a line on a piece of wood with the narrow lead of a number three pencil, telling a fellow worker, "Now, sir, you cut your half of that line and leave me mine." His ability to focus and investigate anything of importance served him in this case. He searched the Elveston farm and found the evidence of a trash fire outside. Pace combed the ashes until he found the remains of the bottle containing strychnine. Interviews in Call and Jasper revealed her purchase of life insurance and poison.

Josie Elveston was every defense attorney's nightmare case: a confession from an unemotional killer, a cold-blooded crime, and a careful and detailed investigation. She spent her days in jail twiddling her thumbs, neither reading nor writing letters, as she waited for the court to appoint her an attorney. One was quickly found.

Joe Tonahill had come to Jasper in 1945. He had attended law school in Washington, D.C., where his roommate was Jasper native Joe Fisher. After a brief spell at the Department of Justice in Washington, Tonahill called his old friend to ask if the invitation to join Fisher in a private practice was still open. Fisher replied, "Come up here and we'll starve together!" The two men quickly developed a busy practice in the small town.

Having Sheriff Pace on the opposing side of a trial was no picnic, though. He was such a credible witness that the only solution was to get him off the witness stand as soon as possible. Pace's humor was also liable to slip out in court as well. Once in a trial, Tonahill put a nervous young man on the stand and calmed him by saying, "Just get up there and tell the truth, son." Pace leaned over and added, "That's right, boy. You can tell the truth the same way a thousand times. But you can't tell a lie the same way twice!"

The Elveston trial was a brief one. Tonahill was able to put up a defense, if a slight one. The toxicology reports showed less than a lethal dose of strychnine in Mr. Elveston's body. By the time the toxicologist testified, he exaggerated the amount, but Tonahill discredited those claims. In addition, the Rangers were forced to admit that they had some unusual interrogation techniques. Holliday promised Josie Elveston that he would buy her a new car if she would just tell the truth about the matter. In the end though, the jury was faced with a clear case of premeditated murder, and the state asked for the death penalty.

The jury adjourned to consider the case around lunchtime. Since the local bar association had planned a meeting for that day, the judge and the attorneys all went out to a nearby ranch for a big barbecue lunch. It was a friendly gathering for the men and they all had a great deal to drink before returning to the courthouse.

When the jury returned, the judge was so drunk he asked them for their judgement (as in a civil case) instead of verdict. Amazingly, Josie Elveston received only a thirty-year sentence, what many considered a virtual acquittal. Perhaps there was still a hesitation to give the death penalty to a woman. A woman of her age may have been a sympathetic defendant. Although she never showed emotion, she looked like anyone's grandmother. Jasper juries did not have much record for giving the death penalty in murder cases. There were usually circumstances that led to reduced charges. Killings often came from family arguments, heat-of-the-moment situations. So this was not entirely a surprise.

All the attorneys left, presumably to sleep off their bar association meeting. The defense attorney was seen afterward at the jail, still inebriated from the bar association barbecue. He had earned the right to celebrate, however. A sentence of thirty years was something of a victory for such a case. Tonahill had achieved the kind of outcome that generates enormous positive publicity for a trial attorney.

The sheriff had finished his work on the case and now had the duty of transporting the prisoner to the state prison for women. He took Viva along for the trip. As they passed through Huntsville, they took a detour by the college there where their youngest daughter was a student. R.C. attempted to locate her on campus so she could meet the notorious Josephine Elveston. Now, most parents of a lovely young daughter try to introduce her to an eligible young man. In the Pace family though, the sheriff and his wife thought it would be interesting to let her meet a convicted murderer! The daughter was in class, unfortunately, and missed her chance.

Following the trial, Mrs. Elveston continued to make her presence known around town. Two weeks after the trial, all of her attorney's files on the case were stolen from his office. It was a mystery what anyone might have gained from the theft, except power of attorney documents. He did not appeal the conviction himself, but a state legislator who was interested in these kinds of cases took up her cause. The man took no fee but he had a well-deserved reputation for success. She was released from prison a mere six years later.

Penniless, she paid a visit to her old attorney. She knew she lacked the money to pay him, but asked for his help in getting her work. Tonahill, whom the sheriff called "Big Joe," could not resist the opportunity for mischief. He sent her to the judge to ask for work as a cook. She returned soon after in a huff - the judge was quite annoyed at Tonahill's suggestion that he hire a known poisoner to prepare meals for the judge who imprisoned her! Tonahill replied that she could consider her bill paid in full. Josie returned to Newton, where her children looked after her until her death.

This was one of the rare crimes in Jasper County that had been committed from a sense of deliberate cruelty. Strychnine poisoning is a horrible way to die, and people may have prided themselves that such a murder was rare in their town. But life was not quiet for long.

The childhood home of R.C. Pace in the Peachtree community of Jasper County.

R.C. Pace and his sister Beulah Pace.

★ ★ ★ ★ ★ ★ ★ ★ ★ ★ ★ ★ ★ ★ ★ ★ ★ ★ ★ ★

Beaver Bishop

R.C. Pace on his horse, taken in front of his home in 1944.

★ ★ ★ ★ ★ ★ ★ ★ ★ ★ ★ ★ ★ ★ ★ ★ ★ ★ ★ ★

R.C.Pace at the jail as he locks up Clayton Rushing in 1947. (Photo by Mac's Studio)

★★★★★★★★★★★★★★★★★★★★

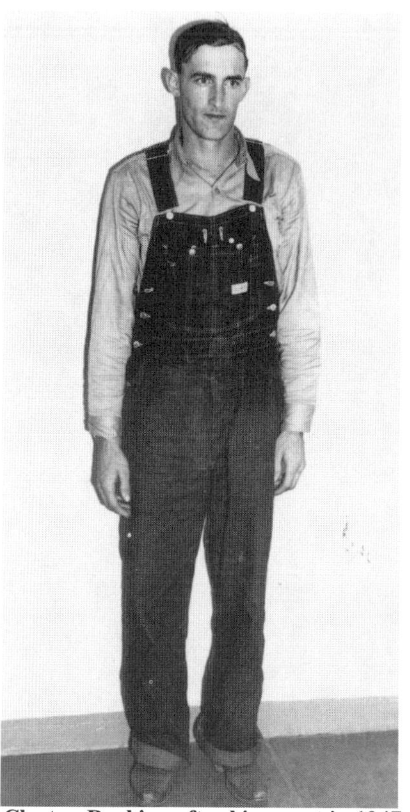

Clayton Rushing after his arrest in 1947. (Photo by Mac's Studio)

R.C. Pace relaxing in the woods.Photo taken around 1948.

Josephine Elveston, seated, as she signs her confession. Standing are (from left) Texas Ranger Dick Middleton, R.C. Pace, Texas Ranger Roscoe D. Holliday.

★ ★ ★ ★ ★ ★ ★ ★ ★ ★ ★ ★ ★ ★ ★ ★ ★ ★ ★ ★

The Pace family in 1952. Seated in front, from left: Mary Pace Mallett, Katherine Pace Baldwin, Viva Pace (holding granddaughter Carol Pace), R.C. Pace, (holding granddaughter Katherine Anne Baldwin), Aileen Pace Smith, daughter-in-law Janie Martindale Pace, Standing, from left: son-inlaw Ned Mallett, son-in law Ray B. Baldwin, Hardy Pace, Jimmy Pace, son-in law Wilton Smith, Robert Pace. Sitting in front are grandsons Bobby Smith and Rip Baldwin.

R.C. Pace returns from hunting deer with son-in-law Ray B. Baldwin, left, and W.D. Baldwin, right. Photo taken around 1950.

R.C. Pace with granddaughter Diane Pace, celebrating his 75th birthday at the jail, 1964.

★ ★ ★ ★ ★ ★ ★ ★ ★ ★ ★ ★ ★ ★ ★ ★ ★ ★ ★ ★

R.C. Pace, center with deputies R.C. Powell (left) and Leonard Franklin (right) in 1955. (Photo by Mac's Studio)

R.C. Pace and Viva (with deputy) serve Thanksgiving dinner at jail, 1963. (Photo by Mac's Studio)

The former Jasper County Jail, now the home of the Jasper County Historical Commission offices and archives. The county courthouse is visible behind building. (Photo by Bertie Bryant)

1947
December

★ ★ ★ ★ ★

Chapter Nine

Woodrow Rushing was a nice, quiet kid. His parents had married late in life and he was close to his mother. She taught him something a bit strange for a boy - crocheting. His classmates said he was good at it, too. So good, in fact, that he helped her make the crocheted bedspreads she sold in town. He was twelve years old in December of 1947 and life was pretty good.

His father, E.J., was a horse trader. They had moved to Jasper from Newton in the previous year. Their three-room house out on the Springhill Road was a simple one. With only a kitchen and two bedrooms, it lacked many conveniences. His mother had no electric iron, and like most women at the time, used smoothing irons. These heavy irons, weighing perhaps six pounds each, were heated on the stove and then used to press their clothes. The family also kept a few hogs on their land. The Rushings were members of the Jehovah's Witnesses, a religious group that anticipated the end of the world would occur soon.

It was a neighbor who first noticed that something was wrong. The Rushings were careful with their hogs, so the neighbors were curious to see them loose. They were wandering the road in search of food, so neighbors sent their son over to tell Mr. Rushing.

The boy knocked at the door but there was no answer, so he peered in the window. A sight more gruesome than he could ever imagine was just inside. There was blood everywhere, and the smell of three bodies that had been dead for several days. The child was traumatized "it put boogers in his head for a LONG time," folks said.

R.C. was quickly summoned. There was no sign of a break-in and the murder weapon was something the killer apparently found at the scene. This led to the assumption that the murderer was someone the family knew. In addition, Pace noticed the ripped nightgown on Mrs. Rushing and the absence of any money in the house. Robbery quickly began to look like the motive. It was not unusual for a woman to pin some valuable to her gown, to a pillow, or under the mattress. Old man Rushing was in a business that was done with cash, and he always had some on hand in case he found a horse he wanted to buy.

Always a sleuth, R.C. continued to survey the dreadful scene. In the barn, he found a new bag of hog feed. Some measuring determined how much had been used. The neighbors described how the hogs had been scavenging for food along Springhill Road, so he knew they had not been fed for some time. A visit to the local feed store revealed that E.J. Rushing had purchased the feed four days before the bodies were found. At the time, he had commented that he was completely out of hog feed.

Pace began to use his network to trace any leads. People were horrified and frightened by the vicious crime, and motivated to tell the sheriff what they knew. Some friends of the Rushing family had waited at the corner nearby to give the family a ride to church the previous Sunday. The Rushings were not there, so the friends drove on. The school reported that young Woodrow had not attended for several days.

While this investigation unfolded, the details of the crime sent a panic through the county. No one knew whether this was a personal feud, or a madman on the loose. R.C. had to contend with anxious relatives who arrived for the funerals. Clayton Rushing was particularly vocal about being kept informed. The sheriff treated the man kindly. Clayton was a World War Two veteran, a son by a previous marriage. Pressure from relatives, however, did not keep Pace from proceeding in his quiet and methodical way.

After two weeks, a very promising suspect appeared. A local truck driver, a black man, had been seen at the Rushing farm on the Thursday before the bodies were discovered. He was someone with whom the family had business. Even more suspicious was the fact that the man suddenly had a bit of money. Jasper was too small a town for someone with money to go unnoticed.

This man was brought in for questioning, but remained calm. He admitted that he had seen the Rushings in the days before their deaths. They had no quarrel, he insisted, and afterwards, he went to Louisiana for the weekend for a big poker game. He told the sheriff that he had been lucky with the cards, and that was the source of his sudden wealth.

For some investigators, there was plenty of evidence to hang the crime on this man. It appealed to the prejudice of so many people at the time. The war had changed some of the most restrictive aspects of racism. A country grateful and proud of its soldiers no longer insisted so forcefully that they move off sidewalks or defer to whites in stores. Still, there was an uneasy distrust that made life hard. The black farmer's son, who Pace called "Little Buck," returned from service in the Pacific, married, and settled down like many veterans. When he went to a local store to purchase a stove, however, he was denied credit, although he had steady work. He paid a visit to the sheriff, who then accompanied the young veteran to the store. With a reference from Sheriff Pace, the man purchased the stove he needed. Even war heroism did not completely bridge the tense racial divide.

This is not to say that Pace was free of prejudice, but rather that he studied people and had a sense of who was honest and who was not. He was comfortable with racial segregation, but his world was split more between the law-abiding and lawbreakers. He left open the possibility that anyone could commit a crime - he had certainly found this in the Elveston case. It was his nature to be thorough and not let his personal feelings cloud his sleuthing ability. In the Rushing case, he tracked down the truck driver's alibi.

To the surprise of some, the alibi held. The man's poker buddies confirmed that he had won at the game, and were still unhappy about their losses. The truck driver, who had been briefly detained in jail, was released. The sheriff found another person close to the Rushings who unexpectedly began to have plenty of money: Clayton Rushing. Pace found that Clayton had accumulated numerous debts, but that immediately after the murders he paid them and began a buying spree. Clayton had an alibi for some days before the bodies were found, but the sheriff's careful study of the hog feed pinpointed a time of death that the alibi didn't cover. A final piece of information was uncovered: a taxi had picked up Clayton in Jasper one evening and had driven him to his wife and child in Newton, precisely on the day Pace determined to be the day of the murders.

Pace had not acted alone in this investigation. He had worked closely with his Ranger friends, R.D. Holliday and Dick Middleton. Before it was over, two other Rangers from Company A (out of Houston) assisted in the arrest.

Clayton had notified the sheriff that he was staying at the home of his father-in-law in Newton County. He said he was there to help the old man butcher some cows. With the Rangers along, Pace could coordinate an arrest outside his own jurisdiction. It was planned to arrest Rushing at daybreak on an icy January morning in 1948. Other family members and acquaintances were to be picked up for questioning at the same time.

The sheriff and one Ranger hid in the woods outside the house. It was bitter cold. When the father-in-law got up, he put on a pot of coffee. Sheriff Pace later said, "That was the best coffee I ever smelled to making."

Finally, Clayton stirred. The sheriff and Rangers blocked both doors to the house and made the arrest. A search afterward turned up the rest of the stolen money buried in a coffee can on the property. In the face of the overwhelming evidence, Clayton Rushing made a full confession. He told the sheriff that had gone to his father's house in the evening. When he arrived, he woke them and they spoke briefly. It was not unusual for him to stay over if he had business in Jasper.

Some time in the night, he began to grow desperate over his financial worries. He had asked his father for money, but the old man had refused to help. The more Clayton thought about it, the angrier he became. Finally, he snapped. He grabbed the smoothing irons and beat his father and then his stepmother. He ripped a cloth bag of cash that Mrs. Rushing kept pinned to her nightgown. The screams woke young Woodrow, and Clayton beat him to death as well, to eliminate any witness.

The trial was held and was sensational enough to make news around Texas. "Inside Detective" magazine sent a reporter, who told the story in a later issue. The deliberate and vile nature of the crime convinced jurors in a way that even Mrs. Elveston's deeds had not. The jury gave Clayton Rushing the electric chair after only twelve minutes' deliberation.

Escorting him to and from the courtroom, Sheriff Pace wore a huge grin for the cameras. There was no sympathy for the killer this time.

Clayton Rushing did not wait long in prison for his execution. Some people claim to have seen a letter he wrote to his insurance company to verify that they would pay life insurance to his family. A minister visited the prisoner, as well. He wrote (with some apparent assistance) a two page letter described as his "Last Written Statement." The letter was heavy with religious language and Bible quotations. In it, Clayton spoke only kindly of his wife and infant son, the jury, Sheriff Pace and others. He added, "I done wrong and I must pay for my wrong with my life." Pace attended the execution.

1948

★★★★★

Chapter Ten

R.C. settled into 1948 with much in life going his way. He had won statewide recognition for his work in the Rushing and Elveston cases and it seemed that the election would be an easy one. County people were unpredictable though, and several challengers forced him to campaign vigorously. One man who ran against him was Forrest Young, who had many supporters and had run against Pace before. Pace was a man who could say his peace in a few words. One recollection of a typical political speech has him saying, "Well, this is old R.C., running again. I like the job. I hope y'all will give it back to me. Only thing wrong with it, it don't pay enough!" This was the entire speech.

This particular campaign must have required more effort. One of Pace's campaign speeches reveals his skill as a politician:

On next Saturday you will select a man to serve you as your next Sheriff. It is your duty, each and every one, to come out and vote.

Every man offering for as important a job as Sheriff should have some record or something to show that he is qualified. Certainly, a man could not give being a quarter boss as experience in law enforcement, for what a company or corporation might permit during a labor shortage to hold their crew, is not the best interest to society.

The Bible speaks of false prophets.

And I warn you that there are some facts that you are being misinformed.

With all sincerity I ask you people if there is any misconduct in my office that brings so much criticism from a few or is it that this few who are hollering so long and loud expects future personal benefits? If so, that is not to the interest of the county or the people.

Now my opponent tried to obligate you people by claiming to be a homeboy. Only a few years ago when he was employed by Alvin Morgan and Charlie Boyington as a jitney driver, he claimed Jasper as his home, and was commonly known by the nickname "Beaumont." Two years ago, when he made an unsuccessful race for sheriff, he was "the bull of the woods from Bessmay." Now when some question of interest to the people comes up, my friend John D. Richardson goes to Tyler County for letters of recommendation. With fairness to both sides, he should publish them all, including the one from their sheriff, a man who knows.

Now it's beginning to look like anywhere he hangs his hat is home.

In his handbill he says he wants the office because it pays a salary. This salary started Jan 1, 1948, and it is the fruit of my untiring effort trying to keep the office on a high plane and free from graft. Now that I spent my money going to Austin in behalf of the law that made this salary possible, I certainly am going to try to draw it two more years.

Now when did he have this change of heart - on Dec. 20, 1947, while all of my time was taken up with the Rushing murder case and I was borrowing help from the state trying to maintain law and order in the county? Two men, Mr. Paul Jordan and Mr. Son Warner from the Liquor Control Board gave me a very unfavorable report of his cooperation. These men work for the state and are not permitted to take sides in politics. However, any of you good citizens who want to vote for your and the county's best interest can call them and they will come and tell you the facts in the case.

I am paying my own campaign expenses and no company, corporation, nor certain group of individuals, is contributing one penny. Therefore, I can do as I have in the past, enforce the law fair and impartial.

In 1941, though in the prime of life, Mr. Young was physically disabled or deferred from serving his country. Now I think it is your duty to give him another deferment and give me the office.

Pace won the election.

The job of the sheriff in a rural county is not only one of law enforcement. No matter what the problem, people often turned to the "high sheriff" for assistance. Sheriff Pace had developed a reputation for fearlessness and was calm in any situation, no matter how bizarre. People said, "He's not afraid of a circular saw."

Pace saw it differently. His strength was in his native ability to understand people, and in particular to understand the way a criminal thought. He had the ability to size up a person's strengths and weaknesses, and the superior mind to out think any crook. Often he fooled a criminal by acting like a dumb country sheriff. When it came to unpredictable situations though, he admitted his fears. He told folks, "There are only three things I am afraid of: a drunk woman, a crazy person, and a stud horse!"

Even in highly unpredictable cases, he was prone to show just how fearless he was. He received a call one day to pick up an elderly man who needed to be taken to the state mental hospital in Rusk. The old man had a gun in his home and Pace wanted to take him into custody as peacefully as possible. Along with a deputy, he drove to the man's farm and walked toward the house unarmed. His plan was to distract the old farmer so that the deputy could grab him. Sheriff Pace walked up to a tree in the front yard and began staring up at the top of the tree and pointing. He continued this odd behavior for a while, until the old man finally came out to the porch to investigate. When he did, the deputy rushed him and tried to tackle him to the ground. Unfortunately, at the same time the farmer's dog ran out of the house and bit the deputy! Pace had to assist his deputy and keep the old man from grabbing his gun at the same time. In this way, they were able to transport the man to the mental hospital without further trouble. This was a situation feared by law enforcement because it had such potential to become tragic. For example, around the same time, an insane man armed with a gun barricaded himself in a building in another Texas town. The Texas Rangers were called out, and law enforcement used an Army tank to capture the man.

Another time, R.C. received a phone call from a distraught family. An elderly man had passed away at home in a remote part of the county. His children wanted to move the body to the funeral home, but their mother had come completely unglued and refused to let anyone into the house. This was typical of a situation that was not exactly a law enforcement issue, but a personal matter that could not be resolved. R.C. took control of the problem at once. He drove out to the house, knocked on the door, and announced himself, "This is Sheriff Pace, ma'am. I sure would appreciate a cup of coffee. I will be waiting for it out here on your porch." After awhile, the woman brought him a cup of coffee and sat with him. Pace spent several hours talking to her. Finally, he was able to calm her and she permitted the rest of the family to take over arrangements for the funeral.

With Hardy graduating from high school, R.C. turned to his youngest boy, Jimmy, for assistance. He began to teach the twelve year-old boy how to drive so that he could drive at night when Pace needed to comb the back roads for a suspect. As the boy grew older, Pace had him assist in arrests. Like his brothers, Jimmy found himself parked outside a house while Pace slipped in the back to make an arrest. Armed with a shotgun, Jimmy waited for the criminal to flee. Sheriff Pace simply told him, "If the fellow runs out the front door, KILL HIM." In one case, the suspect - a wife beater - did come out the front door, but not to escape. Pace had matched his boot to the man's backside and kicked him out of the house. The sheriff had used this method to handle wife beaters for over a decade, and it was still effective. Privately, he complained that he hated to go out on domestic violence cases. All too often, he found himself attacked by both the victim and the perpetrator of violence - an unwinnable situation. More often, if he received a complaint, he called the accused person to meet him at the jail for a discussion. In fact, he often handled cases by a phone call. Most people had the good sense to come when summoned by the sheriff.

Sometimes they did not even wait for a call. There were nights when people appeared late at night at his home. There they confessed to being in a fight and stabbing someone, or beating someone, or some other offense. They knew they were in trouble, and decided to turn themselves over to the sheriff at once. Usually, Sheriff Pace sent them back home with instructions to meet him the following day at the jail. He always found them waiting for him the next day.

These quick confessions were a smart move, even if the Pace family did not enjoy late night visitors. Pace frequently worked favorably with someone who told the truth. If a man could not pay a fine and he had a job, Pace rarely jailed the man. He made arrangements for the man to return to work and pay a small amount each week on payday. Sometimes this meant that a man traveled from another town to see the sheriff every Friday. Criminals knew that he meant business, and anyone who ignored this arrangement faced a much harsher punishment.

In another case, Pace acted behind the scenes for a man convicted of drunk driving. The man had sped north on Highway 96 from Buna to Jasper and was clocked at 110 miles per hour. He was sentenced to serve his time in the local jail. After some months, the man's wife asked Pace to allow him to have an occasional furlough to spend a weekend with his family. Pace permitted this. Few people saw his softer side, but when it came to keeping a family together, the sheriff was willing to make life a bit easier. It was his nature to uphold the law, but as long as a person took responsibility for a crime, Pace never continued to punish the criminal. That is to say, he did not continue to harass someone or act in a vindictive way. If he grew tired of arresting someone repeatedly, he "put the sun on them," giving him the familiar talk. By telling a criminal that his presence was no longer welcome in the county, Sheriff Pace kept many habitual criminals away from his jurisdiction. This generally was successful. Sometimes people who left did not return to the county for twenty years or stayed away forever.

By the election of 1950, Pace thought he owned the county sheriff's position. People were comfortable with him in a way they had not been before with a sheriff. He announced for re-election in late March, promising "the same fair, impartial, conscientious, and fearless enforcement." When campaign time came around, Pace lacked the usual energy for it. His competition was a surprise. His former deputy, (now city marshal) Martell Mixon, found supporters of his own and ran against the sheriff. He ran a hard campaign, going all over the county to persuade people who were already in Sheriff Pace's camp.

Pace led in the primary, held in July. He had 2032 votes to Mixon's 1333, with another candidate, Marvin Richardson, receiving 1142. There were 22,000 residents in the county by that time. It was the only county race that required a run-off election. Mixon continued to campaign aggressively, and it worked. In the August run-off election, Mixon won by 53 votes in a huge upset. Many of Pace's supporters woke the next morning heartsick, but there was nothing to be done. Sheriff Pace was especially furious that many people from his home community of Peachtree had not bothered to vote. He lost Peachtree 54 to 32. He never was known for keeping a grudge, but this one he kept. He announced to all who would listen that he no longer wanted to be buried in the Peachtree Cemetery with his parents and generations of Paces.

There was another factor that may have played into the loss. Many of the young men who returned from World War II were out of Jasper County at election time. Pace's oldest son had gone to Colorado after the war, and many others sought jobs on pipelines and in other industries. Some of his most reliable voters simply were not in town. Another factor must have been the souring of his relationship with his deputy. What goes on between two people who work together can only be theorized. The newspapers, however, show some indication of what might have happened. After the Rushing case, an article in the paper showed Pace thanking the many law enforcement agents who had assisted him: the Texas Rangers, other sheriffs' departments, etc. Only at the end, almost an afterthought, does he show appreciation to his deputy, Martell Mixon. For a seasoned politician, it was a careless mistake to downplay the help received by a local person. Still, Pace retired gracefully, returning to his carpentry work.

Pace had the opportunity at this time to join the Texas Rangers. With his success and extensive favorable publicity from the Elveston and Rushing cases, he was a popular candidate for an appointment. In those days, the Governor of Texas appointed Rangers. His Ranger friends encouraged R.C. to become one of them, but he declined. Jasper was his home and he had no inclination to move.

The year 1950 was not finished with its grief, however. In November, R.C. Pace's dearest friend, Ray Baldwin, passed away from a heart attack. People who attended the funeral recalled that Pace was more devastated than they had even seen him. He did not serve as a pallbearer, but his other close friend, Uncle Jim Hicks, did. Within a week, his friend and colleague, Ranger Roscoe Holliday, also died. It must have been a very low time for Pace. Still, he did not rush to campaign again when the 1952 election came around. Mixon ran unopposed. R.C. had some grandchildren by then, and was enjoying his family and the more regular hours of a carpenter.

He had no trouble finding carpentry work, but began to have worries about his health. Except for his drinking, he generally had good habits and his hardiness and stamina were legendary. Once around this time, he went on a fishing trip with a son-in-law. The two men caught catfish and fried them. They were fried in that soft, slightly underdone way that R.C. liked because he could eat without his false teeth. Afterward, the younger man picked up the pot filled with hot grease to empty it. He lost his grip and spilled the grease into R.C.'s unlaced work boots, which had the flaps lying open. The pain of the burns must have been unbearable, but R.C. endured it. Armed with some whiskey, he drank away the pain until the two men returned to town the following day. The burns were quite severe, and took months to heal.

Still, R.C. had frequent headaches, and began to think privately that he had a brain tumor. He sought treatment at the Scott and White Clinic in Temple, Texas. They found no cancer (which had killed his father and must have been a worry to him). Instead, they discovered his gall bladder was filled with stones and inflammation. He refused surgery, however, and was given a powdered mix to drink that contained bran and other digestive aids. He found this helped him as long as he kept the drinking in check.

In 1954, the old man, by now 63 years old, decided he was not ready to retire. He ran again for sheriff against Mixon. Some people recall this as an ugly campaign, with some unkind and untrue gossip spread about Mixon by Pace supporters. This was not uncommon in local elections. Pace, himself, was accused of various misdeeds. Some of his children had been teased back in the 1940s about their father having a girlfriend. There is no evidence of one, but it was a popular rumor used in political campaigns. Generally the attacks related to his drinking, which he never denied. The year 1954 was not a quiet one for law enforcement. In June, there were three murder trials and Mixon was no doubt busy. Still, people were ready for change and Pace won in the August run-off election: 2936 to 2375. Sheriff Pace was back.

1954
Christmas Day

★ ★ ★ ★ ★

Chapter Eleven

The Pace family settled into a happy family Christmas meal. Their youngest son, Jimmy, was home from college, and R.C. was looking forward to the New Year when he would return to his old job. Viva cooked hearty food like turkey and dressing, ham, vegetables from their garden, and her enormous homemade rolls smeared with butter she had churned herself. The family had just finished this feast when the phone rang. There had been a shooting north of town and, as a courtesy to the incoming sheriff, the county attorney invited R.C. to observe.

The Garlington Ranch was just off FM (Farm to Market) Road 1007, about 15 miles north of Jasper. It was part of the county known as Scrapping Valley, a name acquired from the long reputation it had for feuds. The Garlington family raised exceptional Brahman bulls and other animals on the huge spread. Pace was told that there had been a shootout between members of the Garlington family and a group of deer hunters. R.C. and his son, Jimmy, left at once to take a look at the scene.

Meanwhile, it would be no quiet Christmas at home for Dr. Joe Dickerson, either. He ran the small Hardy Hancock Hospital on the northeast corner of the courthouse square. A group of hunters - members of the Ellis family and their friends - arrived that day for treatment. The elder member of the family, Trav Ellis, had been shot in the head. Another older man, Roy Muench, was dead. The doctor had begun treatment when the other hunters mentioned - almost as an afterthought - that they had left two of the Garlingtons dead in the woods. Dr. Joe, as he was known locally, immediately called authorities.

An ambulance sped to the ranch to retrieve the other victims. To everyone's surprise, Dalphin and Sterling Garlington were still alive, though badly wounded. The Garlingtons' sister, Leola, and other relatives hurried to town.

Soon, the Garlington men arrived for treatment. The doctor had quite an angry group on his hands: hunters upstairs, ranchers and their family downstairs, all with guns. It was a tribute to his skill that he managed to keep the peace and save the lives of Trav Ellis and Dalph and Sterling Garlington.

Up at the ranch, R.C. and his son met up with outgoing Sheriff Mixon and Texas Ranger Harvey Phillips from nearby Woodville. It was apparent that a huge volume of shots had been fired - forty rounds in less that a minute, was one estimate. Branches were shot off trees and it looked like a war zone. Dalph Garlington's Stetson hat was so full of holes, it looked to one observer like a flour sifter. Still, it was Mixon's investigation, and R.C. could only watch.

News soon spread of the dramatic, Old-West style gunfight. A crowd gathered in town. The story was reported in the Houston newspaper and even *Time* magazine sent a reporter.

The Garlingtons were well known to deer hunters. The family had lived in the county for several generations, but held intense dislike for the deer hunters' practice of running hounds through anyone's property. In other parts of Texas, it was a longstanding practice to shoot any dogs that came onto a ranch. A stray dog was always a danger to animals if it carried disease or if it attacked the livestock. In East Texas, hunters resisted any attempt to restrain their activity. The cattle ranchers and their concerns were unimportant. The dogs tracked and the hunters followed. R.C. Pace explained to *Time* magazine in the January 10, 1955 issue: "Five, ten miles ain't no area for a big deer to carry the dogs." He continued, "Once I had one run twelve hours. You can go a long way in twelve hours." The Garlingtons had a reputation for shooting dogs on their land. A local woman commented to *Time* that anyone digging on the Garlington land would find a dog buried every few feet.

In this case, the Ellises had a dog wounded, but not killed. When the hunters found the animal, they drove toward the area where they believed they could talk it out with the Garlingtons. Just how angry they were was not known, although some sources quoted one of them as saying, "The son of a bitch that shot my dog is gonna die!"

The hunters reached a cattle guard in the road and saw the Garlington men, Dalph and Sterling, waiting in a group of trees. They were heavily armed, with a .270 mm rifle, a 12-gauge shotgun and a .44 pistol. According to the hunters, the two older men, Trav Ellis and Roy Muench, got out of their truck. They insisted the younger men stay in the other truck while they talked things out with the ranchers. The Garlingtons opened fire, killing the unarmed Roy Muench. Trav Ellis ducked as they shot and the bullets hit his shoulder and his face, breaking his false teeth. The younger men, Trav's son Charlie Ellis, Clarence Willingham, Richard Morris, and Gerald Sanford, jumped from the other truck and returned fire. They shot Sterling and then chased the other Garlington brother into a field, emptying their guns into him. By the volume of ammunition on the ground, it appeared they may have reloaded and kept shooting. When both Dalph and Sterling were down, the hunters took their dead and wounded to the hospital.

At the hospital, Sheriff Mixon and Ranger Phillips interviewed the hunters and ranchers. Charlie Ellis was a corporal on leave from the Army. Clarence "Shorty" Willingham had been invited to Jasper to hunt with the Ellises. He lived in Beaumont and brought along his father-in-law, Roy Muench. Neither Shorty nor Mr. Muench had ever been to Jasper before. Morris and Sanford were local men.

The interviews did not go well for the hunters. Ranger Phillips was not satisfied with their story. His inspection of the crime scene brought him to conclusions far different from Pace's. Pace believed the hunters in this situation, based on his interpretation of the crime scene and his knowledge of the parties involved. Mixon and the Ranger decided that the shots that killed Muench were not from the Garlingtons. Instead, they suspected that in the confusion, or perhaps intentionally, Shorty Willingham had shot his own father-in-law.

The Garlingtons had long been unpopular with local people. "Isolationist and paranoid" were terms used to describe the family, but they were not paranoid without reason. Back in January of 1941, Pace had briefly hired Cliff Bishop as a deputy. Bishop was the brother of Beaver Bishop. Months later, Pace arrested another man who confessed that he and Cliff had cut the Garlingtons' fence. The man stated that he believed his dogs had been killed by the rancher family, and that cutting their fence "would do some good." Sheriff Pace did not keep Bishop as a deputy. Instead, he received a search warrant from a judge and searched the man's house. There he found the tools used to destroy the fence. Although no records were located, it is likely that charges were filed against the men.

As victims of a shooting, the two Garlington brothers were not sympathetic to any local audience. On this day, however, the Garlingtons found support from Mixon and Phillips. It was a brief investigation and relied heavily on the interviews conducted by Ranger Phillips. Very few photos were taken of the scene. Mixon announced that it was a clear case of self-defense by Dalph and Sterling Garlington. The hunters alone were charged with murder and attempted murder.

Even this did not inspire gratitude by the rancher family. *Time* magazine described a furious Leola Garlington outside the hospital, berating Mixon, "You son of a bitch! It's your fault! If you'd been doing your job, this would never have happened." In the days that followed, Sheriff Mixon returned Roy Muench's body to Georgia for burial. No autopsy was arranged.

The general mood of local citizens was complete astonishment upon the arrest of the Ellises and their friends for the killing of one of their own. People approached Pace at the courthouse square later and asked, "How badly were those Garlingtons shot up?" R.C. just shook his head and drawled, "Not nearly enough!"

1955

★★★★★

Chapter Twelve

When R. C. was sworn in as sheriff after the New Year, he inherited the Garlington case, which was a political hot potato. The shootout was widely reported in Houston newspapers. The Ellises wasted no time in engaging "Big Joe" Tonahill to defend them. The trial took the attention of the public in 1955, but Pace had another agenda. He began to organize the sheriff's department into a more modern law enforcement entity. The days were passing when a sheriff with a couple of deputies (or a teenage son) could handle everything. Mixon, to his credit, had pushed for car radios when he was city marshal. Pace found support from the county to improve radio communication for his department.

First, he had to find some deputies. Here his instincts for people came into play, yet again. He searched for men he knew and decided who he could work with in a cooperative way. While in the past he relied on his sons, they were not the only ones who helped him. From his early days as a sheriff he had the ability to tap into the strengths of others. A local boy with a photographic memory tagged along some nights when he hunted for bootleggers. The boy, whom he called "Bucky," hid beside the road and memorized license plates of cars that took a road near a suspected bootlegger. Sometimes Pace made a large number of arrests on a Saturday night. On Sunday morning he might stop a black man he knew as the man went to church and ask for his assistance. He then had the man count the money the criminals had in their pockets. By having a witness to the search, the sheriff could show that he did not steal from the prisoners. Sheriff Pace trusted the black citizen and in a way this demonstrated an awareness of civil rights concerns before they were a major issue for others in law enforcement. Pace was interested in finding reliable people to assist him, and for him, reliability was an inherited trait.

The Powell family had lived in the community of Holly Springs for many years. They were fond of Pace, and when their son, R.C., was growing up, they joked he had been named for R.C. Pace. In fact, Powell, who was born in 1921, was named for an uncle, but he grew up with great respect for Sheriff Pace. There was also a family connection. Powell was related to the legendary sheriff, Beaver Bishop, Viva Pace's uncle. Powell had a childhood much like Pace's own children, with the responsibilities of many farm chores. The Powells raised mules and hogs and young Powell had little time for anything beyond chores and school. This is not to say that the young people his age were afraid of mischief. A high school football game with Silsbee in the 1938 ended in a riot. Fans attacked each other over a disputed call by the referee. The result of that melee was that Silsbee and Jasper were banned from playing each other for a decade.

R.C. Powell finished high school and attended business college just before World War II. Like many local men, he was sent to distant places during the war. Once it was over, though, he returned to Jasper from the place where he was discharged with no detours along the way, or as he put it, "just as straight as a string." He was working in Newton County in 1955 when Pace approached him to be a deputy. He had no law enforcement experience, but was enthusiastic about working for Sheriff Pace. He began at once, learning on the job by following Pace's lead.

Pace found other men to serve as deputies in Buna and in the south county area in Evadale. With much of the county covered, and new radios and a radio dispatcher hired, the sheriff's department began to change. Prior to having a dispatcher, the jail had often been left unattended. The sheriff often locked the door and left with the prisoners secure, but unguarded, upstairs. This began to change with the new personnel.

R.C.'s department was equipped with a $3300 purchase of car radios, and set out to handle its business. The crimes were familiar ones. In March, a woman was charged with intent to murder her husband. The couple was outside Ralph's Cafe when the woman pulled a .38 caliber pistol on her spouse. Women were on the other side of the courtroom that month, as well. For the first time, they were allowed to serve on juries in Jasper.

When two women jurors could not agree, however, the first such case ended in a mistrial.

The biggest story remained the shootout at the Garlington Ranch and in July of 1955 the trial finally began. There was a standing room only crowd in the courtroom. It was a long trial by Jasper standards: over 15 hours of testimony and 25 witnesses. District Attorney J.L. Smith charged that the hunters had committed an unprovoked attack on the ranchers. They called as their first witness 43 year old Dalphin Garlington.

Dalph claimed that he and his brother, Sterling, heard shooting on Christmas morning and went to investigate just after noon. He stated that they went to the cattle guard on the ranch, armed with a .270 rifle, a 12-gauge shotgun, and a .44 caliber pistol. The cattle guard lay on a private, but county-maintained, road. When Dalph heard trucks approaching, he testified that he and Sterling decided to get off the road. He went up a bank and his brother went into a ditch in the wooded area beside the road. He denied that they were lying in ambush for the hunters.

The hunters arrived in two pickup trucks. According to the newspaper accounts, Dalph claimed he heard the men say, "There go the so-and-so's now." Dalph recognized Charlie and Trav Ellis, and said that one of the Ellis men shot first. The testimony confused newspaper reporters, as some said he blamed Charlie and others said he accused Trav Ellis. The bullet struck Dalph in the hip. Dalph then claimed that he turned and ran, but was shot in the back. He denied that he had ever fired his gun. He said that his sister Leola reached him first, and on cross-examination he denied that she reloaded his gun. His testimony lasted an hour.

Next, Sterling Garlington, Dalph's fifty-three year-old brother, gave his account. He claimed he was in the ditch when Charlie Ellis shot his weapon. Sterling said he suddenly found himself lying on the ground with gunshot wounds to his head and left side. When he turned to his left side, he said, Charlie Ellis shot him in the neck. Sterling denied that he or his brother could have shot first because, he insisted, they could not see the hunters in the thick timber. This contradicted his brother, who claimed to have recognized the Ellises when they arrived at the cattle guard. Dalph had previously testified that he did not ambush the hunters. He admitted that it would have been easily possible, if he had wanted.

For much of his hour on the witness stand, however, Sterling claimed a memory loss about the incident. He did not remember seeing the two trucks. He did not remember firing any shots from his shotgun or from his .44 caliber pistol. His shotgun, with two shells fired from it, was introduced into evidence. The pistol was not.

The biggest witness for the prosecution, Texas Ranger Harvey Phillips, was next on the stand. He testified that he had investigated the scene on the day of the shooting and had interviewed the hunters at the time. Defense attorney Tonahill objected to the interrogation having been held without an attorney present. His objection was overruled and the Ranger spent two hours on the stand, recounting these interviews and identifying the weapons at the scene of the crime. He gave his opinion that the 18 shotgun pellets that entered the body of Mr. Muench entered from above and ranged downward. This indicated to him that only Mr. Willingham, who was in the back of the truck, could have fired the fatal shots. Newspaper accounts never gave any motive for Mr. Willingham shooting his own father-in-law. The victim was only in Jasper County that day because his son-in-law had invited him. If the younger man had wanted to kill Roy Muench, he had opportunities to do so deep in the woods when there were not so many witnesses.

R.C. was called to the stand. He testified briefly regarding the location of the blood spots found at the crime scene The District Attorney only asked him a few questions. Joe Tonahill handled him even more quickly. Pace was not a witness who helped the defense. His deliberate style and authority could, in the attorney's opinion, "bite you like a snake." There were a few points that Tonahill made in his cross-examination of Pace, who confirmed the incomplete quality of the investigation. He agreed that, had he been in charge, he would have ordered that many more photographs be taken of the scene. He also confirmed that he would have ordered an autopsy on Mr. Muench's body. Finally, when asked if he would have filed charges on all the participants, not only the hunters, Pace replied, "I think I would."

The defense called all five hunters to the stand. They all denied that they had been "looking for trouble," and insisted that they had shot in self-defense after being fired upon by the Garlington brothers. The men claimed that when they arrived at the cattleguard, they blew their horns to get the other dogs to return. At this point, they testified, Dalph began swearing and threatening them. All of the hunters insisted that Sterling, and not "Shorty" Willingham, had fired the shots that killed Roy Muench and wounded Trav Ellis. They identified the location of Mr. Muench as being twenty-five feet from where Sterling Garlington was hiding in the ditch.

The next defense witness also refuted the testimony of Ranger Phillips. Doctor Joe Dickerson, who treated all the men on the day of the shooting, insisted that the shots which entered Mr. Muench's body came from a parallel level, and not from above and angled downward.

Finally, the defense called a string of witnesses who testified to the "gun-toting viciousness" of the Garlingtons. There were many local hunters available to speak to this reputation, but the defense presented a list of very reputable men. A high school teacher, a local contractor, and other solid citizens described being chased, often at gunpoint, off the Garlington Ranch when they went there to search for missing dogs.

The attorneys rested their case and the jury began its deliberations at 9:52 p.m. on a Monday night. They reached a verdict in less than an hour. The clerk read it just as the courthouse clock struck eleven. The jury was not convinced by the account given by Garlington brothers. They found nothing to indicate that Clarence Willingham or any other hunter had fired the fatal shots that killed Roy Muench. All the hunters were found not guilty. Trav Ellis cried in relief as the verdict was delivered. Other charges that were pending against the hunters were dropped for lack of evidence. The rest of that year was quiet, but the case of the hunters and ranchers was not forgotten.

In August, soon after the trial, country music singer George Jones played a police benefit at a local skating rink. Jones had a long history of arrests in Jasper, times when he had gotten drunk and made trouble. Eventually, Sheriff Pace "put the sun on him," telling him the familiar lecture. He made it clear to Jones that his presence was not welcome in the county as long as Pace was alive. When R.C. was out of office in 1954, Jones was once again arrested in Jasper. Perhaps as part of his sentence, he agreed to play a benefit concert. He was not arrested in town again.

A couple of juvenile delinquents passed through town in late September. They stole a car and robbed the snack bar at the local drive-in theatre. Their take included twenty cases of barbecue meat, fifteen cartons of chewing gum, a vending machine's worth of cigarettes, and a check for $27.50. They cashed the check on their way out of town and were later caught in Oklahoma.

Other than a few incidents, life settled down for the time being. R.C. still found time to get away to the woods to hunt deer. Like many in the county, he hunted almost year-round in defiance of the legal season which began in the late fall. Some claimed the sheriff's hunting season began on July 5th, when he could shoot the young "popeyed" deer which he enjoyed eating. On one trip, he took the son of one of his friends. The young man was sitting on some abandoned railroad tracks when he saw a young deer prance by. Right behind the deer, came R.C. He was carrying a rope and trying to lasso the deer! There was no way to know what Pace would do next.

1956

★★★★★

Chapter Thirteen

The New Year brought a new grand jury. In February, the Garlingtons were indicted for murder. In addition, an autopsy was ordered on the victim, Roy Muench. Sheriff Pace prepared to set off for Georgia where Muench was buried in order to complete the task.

Before he left, he received information from the FBI that a bank robbery gang might be in his area. He and some other men rode the back roads by night, and hid on the banks of the Neches by day, in search of the gang. One day while they were at the river, a man drove by. When he saw the sheriff's car, he sped up. This made the men suspicious and they followed him. He headed east of town and tried to cross a railroad track too quickly. His car hung on the "frog" - the switch on the track. The man jumped from the car and took off into the woods. Sheriff Pace and the men followed him with their bloodhounds.

As a rule, bloodhounds are not aggressive. A scratch behind the ears could quiet them. R.C. kept hounds at his Newton Highway home back in the 1930s. The animals were so nervous that whenever there was a thunderstorm, they broke out of their pen. He did not keep them for long.

On this day, the dogs were on loan from the state prison in Huntsville. The stranger was terrified of the dogs and quickly surrendered. He had a good reason to worry. At that time, law officers might put a "catch dog" in with the hounds. This dog was not trained to follow, but to attack a fugitive viciously.

Pace and the other men brought the stranger back to jail. In the beginning, there were no charges. His suspicious behavior, however, convinced R.C. that he was guilty of something. The man, who was white, had somewhat long and stringy hair. One of Pace's friends decided he needed a haircut, and proceeded to yank the man's hair out by the handful. The man grew more cooperative after that.

R.C. slowly began to ask the man questions. While the license plate was being checked (a much longer process in those days), he was gradually able to trip the man up on his answers. The more the men learned that this stranger was in trouble with the law, the less they felt like being polite. The hair pulling was probably only part of it. In a way, the man was lucky that there was no catch dog. Lawmen did not object if the dog gnawed the clothes (or perhaps the flesh) off a suspect in those days.

The whole story finally came out. The man, Marvin Falls, had been in prison in Arizona, where he was serving time for car theft and burglary. One day, he sawed his way out and then stole five automobiles as he traveled from Arizona to Oklahoma to Texas. He still had the hacksaw in his shoe. He might have stayed free for a long time, except that his path led him through Jasper County.

In May, Pace began the trip to Georgia. Normally, when he drove somewhere, he arrived in a hurry. He was a notoriously fast driver. One day, when he and a deputy had driven Viva out to their house after she delivered meals for the prisoners, Pace sped through a stoplight. Viva began to scream, "You ran a red light! You ran a red light!" Pace was unconcerned. "Hush up, Viva," he growled. "I've got a license to drive this car and I had to DRIVE to get it!" If Pace wanted others to hurry, he often said, "It's time to shake Kittie Tom!" One of his children said he always understood this to mean, "an old cat - Kittie Tom - could run fast if it HAD to." Pace used the phrase often and many people associated it only with him. No one else, apparently, used this unusual expression locally but R.C. Pace.

But on this trip to Georgia, there was not as much need to hurry. Travelling with R.C. were city attorney Ward Markley, Dr. Joe Dickerson, Dr. Dickerson's cousin, Barber Dickerson (the town barber),and Texas Ranger Harvey Phillips. From the outset, the men argued about their different views on the case. Markley and others drove, and Sheriff Pace surprised them with a request. As they entered each new county on the way, he insisted that they stop at the courthouse so he could meet the local sheriff. On these visits, he asked about salaries, cars, and other benefits in the sheriffs' departments. Because of the "courthouse tour," the drive to Georgia took longer than expected. The men stopped for the night in Alabama, near the border of Georgia.

At the hotel that evening, the men ate and drank and talked. There was a group of college boys in the hotel lobby, and Barber Dickerson took them aside. "Watch out, boys," he told them. "That there is a Texas Ranger and a sheriff with a couple of real desperadoes!"(meaning the doctor and the county attorney). The college boys were so excited, they mobbed the lawmen. They wanted to handle Pace's gun, his badge, and everything he was wearing. His friends thought they might undress the sheriff in their excitement.

After a while, the men went up to their rooms. Doctor Dickerson was not asleep for long when he heard a knock on the door. It was R.C., looking very worried. He told the doctor, "I believe those college boys stole my gun! I can't find it and I think we should sound the alarm." They returned to Pace's room, where Ranger Phillips was sleeping. The doctor woke him and told him the gun was missing. The Ranger just looked at the men and said, "Well, you might want to look under his pillow first, because that is where I saw him put it!" Pace found the gun under his pillow and was quite embarrassed. Now it was his turn to be the object of ridicule. His friends teased him about losing his weapon for a long time afterward.

The men arrived in Georgia the next day, completed the autopsy, and returned quickly to Jasper with the eighteen shotgun pellets from Roy Muench's body.

Now it was the Garlington brothers who needed an attorney. As ranchers, they must have developed a deep appreciation for reliable quality, because they initially tried to hire Joe Tonahill to defend them. He was only too happy to explain that it was a conflict of interest. After all, his clients, the Ellises and their friends, were to be the chief witnesses against the Garlingtons. The rancher family hired the services of Wardlaw Lane and Ben Ramsey, two experienced trial attorneys, instead. By June of 1956, attempts were made to set a trial date. Several witnesses were unable to appear around that time, so the case was continued.

The summer passed with only a handful of criminal cases, but eighty-two divorces, in the small town. Martell Mixon again ran in the primary election against Pace. Pace was victorious, 3284 votes to Mixon's 2214.

The town was changing in subtle ways. The rural community in which children swam in creeks now decided to build a public swimming pool. The newspaper widely publicized the effort to raise money for the pool through donations. School children took up collections and citizens were convinced of the good sense of a well-maintained pool where children could learn to swim properly. No mention was made of the fact that the "public" pool was meant only for the white citizens of the county.

A new law came into effect at this time that also showed the way the town was transforming from a rural farm community into a modern town. It had been common practice throughout the town's history for livestock to graze wherever they wanted. The courthouse square often had a few cows or hogs in residence. With the passage of a new stock law, people were required to contain their animals. Two deputies were hired to enforce this law throughout the county.

One of the stock deputies, Estus Miller, had spent many years raising horses. Miller's family was from Browndell in the north part of the county. He had known and respected R.C. Pace for most of his life. Although the job mostly involved rounding up stray animals, Miller had to be prepared to assist the sheriff whenever necessary. To Miller, Sheriff Pace was just a natural born lawman - he possessed skills that were impossible to teach. The sheriff tried to pass those skills on to his deputies as best he could. The old sheriff explained the job in this way:

> *"Miller, I've known you all your life. I knew your mother and daddy ahead of you. Being a lawman is like riding balky horses. As long as you're about half scared of the horse, you ain't going to get bucked off. That's the same with a man.*
>
> *When you go to arrest a man be sure you have your pistol. Don't shoot him unless you have to. Treat him like you'd like to be treated, and you won't never have no trouble."*

The sheriff's advice was timeless, but the dangers faced by the town were changing. Juvenile crimes were growing increasingly common. In contrast to modern sentencing laws, in the 1950s, juveniles were sentenced for delinquency, not the actual crime. In one case, a fifteen-year-old black girl stabbed a man in the chest and stomach, killing him. She was not charged with murder, only delinquency. Other juveniles stole guns or destroyed property.

Still, the biggest danger for people had to be on the highways. There were seven highway deaths that year. Crime statistics show that every month there were arrests for drunkenness or for being drunk in a car (separate offenses). Jasper County residents were fond of fast driving, as well. One week in June, the police gave 119 speeding tickets.

The year ended with the Garlington trial still on hold. It was a drought year, which ended with a 2 1/2-inch downpour in December. There was one mysterious death. A black man, Cleburn Adams, forty-six, was found dead in the Neches River. The newspapers reported that Sheriff Pace was investigating. It was not mentioned again.

1957

★ ★ ★ ★ ★

Chapter Fourteen

R.C.'s home life was disrupted once again by a family tragedy. There was a nationwide polio epidemic at this time. The small town was waiting for the new vaccine that had recently been approved. It did not arrive soon enough. One of Pace's grandchildren contracted the illness. Treatment was long and time-consuming, and Pace, now sixty-six, took in the child's infant sister so the parents could concentrate on their sick child. R.C. always adored babies, and this was an unexpectedly happy situation for him and Viva. They still had frequent help at the house from some of the prisoners, so this granddaughter enjoyed the experience of being looked after by 'jailbirds' like the previous generation had.

As the Supreme Court ruled that segregated schools were unconstitutional, many white Southerners began to scramble to find ways to resist change. In January, a White Citizens' Council meeting was announced in the local paper. The group described its purpose as the defense of segregation laws. It was a time of segregated schools, segregated bathrooms, and even segregated cemeteries. The local movie theatre had a separate balcony entrance for blacks. Before enforced busing became a controversial way for schools to be integrated, East Jasper whites routinely bused their children miles past the Rowe Elementary School (a black school) to reach the all-white Parnell Elementary on the west side of town.

Still, the town maintained a quiet cordiality between the races. While some citizens worried about integration, the local Kiwanis Club (a white service organization for men at the time) donated a wheelchair to a young black man who had polio. The young man, a high school graduate despite his disability, was photographed with local Kiwanis Club members by the local newspaper.

Violent crime continued to occur mostly within families in Jasper. A black woman was attacked by her husband, who used a double bit ax in a brutal assault. The man, forty-one-year old Louie Smith from Newton, had an extensive prison record. He had also attacked his wife three weeks earlier with a pistol. He tried to persuade her to drop the previous charges and that argument led to this incident. He was caught near the railroad tracks. Some claim that the man's life had been spared only because R.C. tripped as he fired his weapon at the man.

The town police still had to deal with poor drivers. They complained in the summer of stop sign violations. In one week, twenty-one people were cited for running stop signs. By the year's end, there were thirteen highway deaths.

The tradition some Jasper people had for stealing anything imaginable reached a new high that summer. Thieves stole a bridge from a private road down in Buna. It was dismantled and sold for parts in nearby Lufkin. Jasper was often a target of outsiders, too. That year, three armed robbers held up the clerk at a local motel, the Holton Motor Court. Two Oklahoma teens who had escaped from reform school were caught committing burglaries. Then in July, three teenagers from Nederland, Texas, were arrested for stealing thirteen cows.

The Garlingtons were finally brought to trial after a long delay. Their attorney, Wardlaw Lane, had received a continuance while he served in the state legislature. He then successfully managed to have the trial moved to nearby San Augustine. The autopsy produced no substantial new evidence and the conflicting stories of the witnesses remained unresolved. Lane and Ben Ramsey were highly skilled and the San Augustine jury acquitted the Garlington brothers. Neither the Jasper nor the Houston newspapers, which had been so involved in reporting the first trial, mentioned the disappointing verdict. Perhaps they were sidetracked by a fierce flu epidemic that struck in early September. With over 25% of students ill, the schools closed for a week around the same time as the trial.

R.C. was not finished with his bad feelings toward the Garlington family. Sometime after the trial, Pace and his son-in-law were hunting in the Scrapping Valley area with three hounds. A blue-tick hound named Annie returned with a bullet hole through the hollow of her neck. The other hounds did not return. Pace was enraged. "I'd love to be looking at the man that put that bullet hole right there," he told his son-in-law. Back in town, he frightened his deputies with his anger. It happened that Dalph and Sterling Garlington were out of the area at the time of the incident. Their brother and sister, however, were home. Sheriff Pace could not find enough evidence to prove who had shot old Annie, but his deputies were absolutely convinced that he was angry enough to kill that person. In time, he let the incident pass.

By 1958, Pace had received a pay raise. He now made $5280 per year. He certainly earned it with his around-the-clock work. He continued to impress his young deputies with his stamina. Around this time, someone was robbing homes by cutting the screens on the windows and sneaking in late at night. R.C. stayed up many nights trying to catch the man, without success. One night, Pace dreamed the man cut the screen next to his bed. The following morning, he found that it was no dream - his screen was indeed cut. The man was lucky he had not entered the Pace home, for it is unlikely he would have survived the visit. Pace still kept his pistol underneath his pillow. The burglar quit soon after, and was never caught. Pace preferred to catch a criminal as soon as possible. He often told his deputies, "The longer a fox is gone, the harder he is to trail."

Sometimes, Pace did not trail the criminal at all. He knew every inch of the county and still had a keen detective mind. When the local Suzie Q service station was broken into, the burglar stepped in a pan of old motor oil and left his size fourteen shoe print on the concrete floor. Pace sat at his desk for several weeks after. He propped one foot on the desk and crossed the other ankle over his knee. He took out his pocketknife, which hung from a chain, and tapped the ends of the knife on the desk back and forth, back and forth. Finally after a few days, he told his deputy, "That man that broke into that station he stepped in that oil with his right foot. He's asleep somewhere, and his shoes are under his bed. I believe I know where his bed is." He and the deputy then went to a house where they found the man with the oil-stained shoes and made an arrest.

1958

★ ★ ★ ★ ★

Chapter Fifteen

Modernization continued in Jasper County as it did in much of the country in the late 1950s. R.C., now two decades from his first election, seemed to adapt smoothly to this change. His keen political instincts and his reputation were still strong. He had the ability to enter into the most volatile situation and exit it unharmed. He calmed people with his folksy demeanor and his innate authority. One person insisted that Sheriff Pace never found himself in need of his weapon, because he could "manipulate with his lips" any hostility. One son described the sheriff's talent by saying, "He knew when to and when not to." The deputies learned on the job by watching him. In one earlier instance back in the 1940s, Pace had sent a deputy to arrest a local man who was known by the nickname "Nuts." The deputy made the mistake of letting Nuts go into his house alone before taking him to jail. The deputy stood outside as Nuts went in the front door and slipped out the back into the woods. Sheriff Pace was not surprised by the escape. He told his deputy, "There is no need to go out. It's just like looking for a boar hog in a berry patch - we won't find him!" Nuts was gone for some time, but sent the sheriff postcards from out of state.

When the sheriff hired a deputy to a permanent assignment in Buna, in the south part of the county, he advised the man that the town had two groups with political influence. These were informal cliques, formed by kinship and not actual organizations. Pace told the man not to favor either side, but to form his own alliances in the small community. The deputy took his advice and did well there for a while. Unfortunately, the man involved himself in a romantic relationship that created a scandal and he resigned.

Early in 1958, some of Pace's deputies found themselves in deeper trouble. R.C. Powell and Alton Wright had assisted Sheriff Curtis Humphreys in neighboring Newton County in an arrest. They took a black man into custody and during the investigation, apparently used considerable physical force with the man. Some people later claimed that the lawmen arrested the wrong person, which may explain the unusual step the arrested man took next. He filed a federal lawsuit against the deputies and the Newton sheriff for violation of his civil rights. These cases were rare and only beginning to be heard in federal courts.

Pace supported his men in a way that won their admiration. One of his deputies complained in later years that others in law enforcement would withdraw from a fellow officer in legal trouble. As he put it, they would "run backward like a mule hit with a bridle." Sheriff Pace, however, was dependable. People said he was "a man you could ride the river with," or that "You could take his word to the bank." In this case he remained loyal and defended his deputies to outsiders.

The trial was held in Beaumont and the lawmen, defended by the able counsel of Joe Tonahill, were all found not guilty. Sheriff Pace was never sued, but he certainly paid careful attention to the case and it affected his decisions in the years ahead.

A black man was shot one night in a dance hall and barbecue restaurant on Huff Creek. A few days later, another black citizen Sheriff Pace knew well came to the jail. He told the sheriff that he knew the man who was responsible for the shooting. This was a typical example of Pace's strength as a sheriff. People trusted him completely and gave him information. The suspect in this case was the son of a local civil rights leader. The informant swore that the person he named had shot the man and had thrown his gun off a bridge into Millum Creek. Upon hearing this, Sheriff Pace was cautious. He considered the informant's story and then responded. "I've known you a long time, and you've been a big help to me, but if we don't mind, we might get off in some water that might be too deep to wade," – that is to say, if he went after the wrong man, there would be political trouble. The man just replied, "No, sir, Sheriff, if I tell you it's raining, call your dog in, because he'll have some water on him."

Based on this information, Pace and a deputy drove to the home of the suspect's father. The sheriff asked the father politely to see his son. The old man asked why, and Pace only said, "I want to talk to him a few minutes." The father looked concerned and said, "If there's anything wrong, I want to know it." Pace assured him, "If there's anything wrong, I'll bring him back in a little bit and tell you what's wrong."

The two lawmen put the young man in their car and drove away. The three rode in silence. Pace drove with the suspect beside him in the front seat. The deputy sat in the back. This type of driving around with a suspect was sometimes called "automobile custody."

When they arrived on the bridge of Millum Creek, Pace turned to his suspect and said, "You shot that boy over at that dance hall. I know you threw that gun in the creek. Now, the only thing I don't know is what side you threw it in on - but the sooner you get it, the sooner we'll clear all this up." Upon hearing that, the suspect got out of the car and dove into the creek. The second time he dove off the bridge, he came up with the gun. R.C. and his deputy took him to jail.

Some days, Pace had only to sit in his office at the jail and trouble found him. The jail was next to the courthouse on the square downtown. At that time, the local funeral parlor was across the street to the east. The court occasionally required the funeral director, Mr. Stringer, to bury indigent persons. The county paid this expense but was not always prompt. Mr. Stringer complained once to the county judge. Soon after, the judge decided to pay a visit to the funeral parlor when there was a funeral in progress. He burst in, drunk and loud, and proceeded to berate Mr. Stringer with a string of colorful and unprintable words. It was a shocking scene and very disturbing to the family who was grieving there.

The next day, Mr. Stringer paid a visit to the sheriff to complain. "That judge came in drunk," he told Sheriff Pace. "He threatened me! What should I do?" Sheriff Pace just sat in his chair and drawled, "Well, just SHOOT the son of a bitch!"

In 1959, Jasper made another transition when the last big sawmill in the town burned. This was a hard, economic blow to the community that eliminated many of the jobs that supported workers who had little education. An earlier sawmill camp that had once housed more than five hundred workers was now a country club and golf course. For those with skills or a business, though, the town reflected increased prosperity. Newer and more elegant homes appeared in the west part of town, near the white schools. Within a few years, the building of Sam Rayburn Dam brought more highly skilled people to the community and the population grew.

The traditional pastimes did not fade, however. Hunting still went on around the clock and in all seasons. Late one night around this time, a group of hunters became lost in the woods. When they were found, their friends presented them with a cowbell so that others could find them the next time they were lost. Hunting at night was popular, and Pace, himself, got lost one night on Sherwood Creek. When relatives began to worry, they sent out a young man to find the hunters. When the young man found Pace and his friends, Pace persuaded him to go into the woods to help them bring out a deer they had killed. The young man managed all this by staying up all night. By daybreak, he brought the old men home and then left for work.

Pace still enjoyed his job and his attention did not seem to fade with age. When people asked his wife how long the old sheriff would stay on the job, she told them, "As long as he can put one foot in front of the other." He continued to show the stamina of a much younger man and his ability to notice the smallest detail remained strong. One day, he was out east of town looking for some of his cattle. He had several deputies helping him, and they rode on horseback in tall sage grass. The horse that Pace rode grew balky and threw him to the ground. His deputies watched in amusement as the numerous pens and pencils that he kept in his pockets fell into the grass. Pace was not hurt, but he was determined to retrieve the contents of his pockets. He went to town and fetched a few prisoners from the jail. Returning to the field, he instructed the prisoners to pick up all the pens and pencils they could find. To the surprise of the deputies, Pace kept the men looking for a long time, as he knew exactly what he had in his pockets. The deputies could only laugh as the watched the prisoners searching and searching until Pace was satisfied that all the contents of his pockets had been found.

The sheriff continued to teach the deputies by his example. One prisoner, a young man, gave the deputies a hard time. He refused to eat and when they gave him food, he kicked the plate under the cell door. Sheriff Pace told his men, "Let me feed him. I think I can put him to eating." He then let the man go without food for two days. Sheriff Pace took an empty tin plate to the prisoner, keeping the food outside the cell. He looked at the young man and quietly said, “Now, hold your plate down here and I’ll give you some groceries.” The prisoner held the plate still as the sheriff raked on some food. There was no more trouble. Sheriff Pace later told his men, “I done one of my boys that way one time, when he didn’t like the way Mama was cooking his eggs.”

Life was fairly easy for him at this time, with reliable deputies and a peaceful home life. Many of his children stayed in the county and he now had more time to enjoy his grandchildren. One year, he and Viva drove to California to see new grandchildren, but they otherwise stayed close to home. He never lost an understanding of how difficult the lawman’s life could be. He continued to be the man that people turned to with almost any difficulty. He still drank heavily, but never lost the respect of his deputies. One of them said, “I’ve seen him work when he was so drunk he couldn’t put his boots on the right feet, and I’d just as soon work for him DRUNK as work for him sober.”

1960

★★★★★

Chapter Sixteen

Jasper eased into a new decade with R.C. still comfortable in the office he had held for so many years. The county had grown from just over 20,000 in 1950 to 22,100 in 1960. There was little change in the crimes that he and his deputies handled. Deadbeat dads (who failed to pay child support) went to jail and one of the biggest cases that year involved cattle theft. Sheriff Pace was 69 years old and finally growing tired of the politics of the job. He complained around this time about district attorneys who failed to win convictions. "I don't mind the work," he told friends. "I LIKE to work, but by God, I want RESULTS!"

Still, Pace ran for office again. His opponent was once more Martell Mixon, who Pace beat 2657 to 2311 votes. 1960 was memorable in Jasper for a big snow that closed the local schools. For the sheriff, it was a sad time when he lost his old friend Uncle Jim Hicks. Despite his advanced age, Pace served as a pallbearer. He again reminded his family how he had not forgotten his grudge against the Peachtree community. He insisted that he wanted to be buried in the cemetery in town, near his friends Ray Baldwin and Hicks. This may not seem like an unusual request, but for that county, it was. A man who descended from one of Jasper's pioneer families was expected to have a grave near his parents and grandparents. The Paces were buried in Peachtree. Sheriff Pace had the right to be buried there for free, but he insisted that it was his choice to be laid to rest in town in a cemetery far from his ancestors. He was still an active man and no decision was taken at that time.

The Lazy Acres Motel opened in town that year. It had not been in business long when Pace received a call from a West Texas sheriff he knew. The lawman was looking for an escaped convict who was believed to be in Jasper. A few phone calls later, Sheriff Pace located the criminal at the Lazy Acres. The sheriff called one of his deputies at home late at night and told him, "We've got a bad dude. I had a call from a sheriff who has been a lot of help to me, so we have to get him." The two men drove to the motel and found the room where the man was staying. The man had committed numerous violent crimes. The deputy was so afraid that he later insisted that he had "goosebumps as big as marbles" just remembering the criminal.

Sheriff Pace remained completely at ease. He knocked on the door of the motel room and identified himself as the sheriff. He told the man, "I've got a warrant for your arrest. Now, I didn't get you into the trouble you're in, but you get up and put your clothes on and go with me and I'll help you get out of it if I can. But," he added, "you don't want to get in trouble over here in my county, because I'm the only one that's elected. The rest of them are hired." He let the man know that only the sheriff would answer to the public if there were trouble.

The man called out from inside the room, "No, I'm not coming out there." Sheriff Pace stayed calm. Instead of forcing his way in, he quietly told the man, "Well, open the door a little bit, let me talk to you." The man opened the door and Pace stuck the toe of his boot in the door to keep it open. The sheriff wore a large gold pocket watch on a chain. He pulled out his watch and stared at it so the man could observe him. Then the sheriff told him, "I was afraid I was going to have trouble with you. I stopped by the funeral home tonight on my way here. I told them to call their ambulance driver. I said that if I didn't come back in about 15 minutes to come out to Lazy Acres, there'd be somebody to haul back." Then Pace was quiet for a moment. The convict picked up his suitcase and surrendered. R.C. and his deputy took the man to jail without further trouble.

In 1961, the sheriff's work did not change that much. One Sunday morning a car was stolen in front of the First Baptist Church during services and a thirteen-year-old boy was arrested. These juvenile criminals must have bothered the seventy-year-old sheriff. There were cases of child desertion that always disturbed the sheriff's sense of duty to family. One energetic group of thieves stole 3240 pounds of copper wire. They carried it to Lufkin and sold it for $486. Another citizen was arrested for obstructing a public road - the man built a fence across it. In one unexpected case, a black teacher was charged with excessive beating of a pupil. The schools were still segregated by race at this time, but physical punishment was common and acceptable to most parents. In this instance, it was surprising that a parent would even bring charges against a teacher. The teacher was acquitted.

The local district attorney began to complain loudly in the local newspapers about the sheriff's office. He insisted that the sheriff was not working hard enough to close down bootleggers and local dance halls (called "honky-tonks") that were run by black citizens. The publicity over these complaints even began to effect Pace's family. One of his grandchildren was teased at school, which infuriated the protective sheriff. He paid a visit to the district attorney and told him to complain to him directly and leave his family out of the situation.

Pace's troubles were not too exciting, which could not be said for his old deputy and regular opponent, Martell Mixon. Mixon was now working in Houston. While he was driving in downtown Houston one day, some black men sped past in a car and hurled insults his way. Both cars pulled into a parking lot and the men got into an argument. Mixon drew his gun to hit the man in the face. He claimed later that the gun fired accidentally, killing the young black man. Newspaper accounts at the time said the dead man's friends were too drunk to give statements. No charges were filed against Mixon.

The local schools briefly became shelters in 1961 when Hurricane Carla struck the Texas coast and thousands of coastal residents came to Jasper seeking shelter. The town itself suffered no damage, but life was dramatically changed for a brief time with schools closed to handle a rapid increase in the population.

Courthouse staff arrived in the county tax office one morning in 1962 to find that it had been robbed. They may have thought it was a secure building, housing, as it did, all the legal records of the small town. The burglar was caught when he returned to try to rob again. It turned out not to be a local man, but someone from Florida. It was a busy year all around for crime. Sheriff Pace reported early in the year that he had a full jail – twenty-four prisoners. He commented that it had been a long time since he had

had a capacity crowd. The sheriff's office was given new Ford automobiles and they certainly needed them. In Kirbyville, graves were vandalized in what was described as a "sadistic" way. In the summer, a man kidnapped his wife and children. Fortunately, he released them unharmed. A black woman was arrested for killing a man with both an axe and a knife. There was another brutal murder that year, as well. A seventeen-year-old white boy killed a man during an apparent robbery attempt in a store. There seemed to be a wave of juvenile crime. Two Baytown boys, ages twelve and thirteen, were arrested for car theft. There were teenaged runaways taken into custody, as well. In another crime, small wall unit jukeboxes were stolen. There were armed robberies, and cows were killed. In such a climate, local juries were in a mood to send the criminals away, but it was not always the case. The seventeen-year-old killer claimed that the store owner had made sexual advances to him, and that he had "blacked out" and did not recall the crime. The jury did not buy it and gave him 99 years. However, in a different situation, a local black man with a reputation for bootlegging was arrested for making threats against the local justice of the peace. The jury found him not guilty.

The sheriff's old friend Ranger Phillips from Woodville died in 1963. Phillips, who had argued the Garlington case with R.C. but had kept a friendly working relationship, had suffered a terrible personal tragedy. He was driving on an unfamiliar road when his car crossed a railroad track and was hit by a train. He and his son survived the crash, but his wife and daughter were killed. He turned to a familiar attorney, Joe Tonahill, and in a civil suit, received a substantial settlement from the railroad. Once Ranger Phillips knew that his son was financially secure, he retreated to his home alone. He was later found dead from a self-inflicted gunshot to the head.

The autumn of 1963 is one that many Americans remember with sadness. In Jasper, a crisis had erupted early. The old Pep Hotel, a downtown landmark for many years, burned to the ground in October. The blaze brought out the whole town to watch. Then the next month, the assassination of President Kennedy stunned the community, as it did the world. There is no doubt that Sheriff Pace would have been eager to join any investigation of the crime in his home state. Viva told their family and friends that she received calls from people asking if her husband would be assisting law enforcement in Dallas. He was never asked, but he quietly stayed in touch with his friends who were. His family recalls that R.C. knew information long before it was reported in the newspapers. Still, life continued normally for the family, and at Thanksgiving there was a photo in the local paper of R.C. and Viva serving Thanksgiving dinner to the prisoners.

1964

★ ★ ★ ★ ★

Chapter Seventeen

In January, R.C. celebrated his birthday. He was seventy-three, and had privately told his deputies that he would retire, so the occasion was celebrated with a cake and numerous photos in his office.

R.C. Powell had been approached many times to run for sheriff. Local people had begun to approach him after he had been a deputy four years. He refused, telling them, "That ain't the deal. I'm gonna run for sheriff when this man takes a notion to retire. And I'm not gonna run until then." He never had any interest as long as Sheriff Pace was in office. His respect for the old sheriff was life-long, and when Pace decided he was finished with the job, he told Powell, "You get ready to run this time, cause I'm not gonna run anymore."

Pace spoke to reporters when he made his retirement announcement and clearly showed his fondness for Powell. He even went so far as to claim that the deputy was his namesake, although that had only been a joke that the Powell family told.

For Viva, the notion of her husband's retirement gave her some brief optimism. She longed to travel and her health was still quite good. One day around this time, she was cleaning a bookcase at the top of the stairs in their home. When she stood on a chair, she lost her balance and tumbled headfirst down the stairs. She and R.C. decided that she was not seriously injured and she did not even call a doctor. The next day, Viva awoke to find that her arm was swollen to the size of a watermelon. She had broken her arm and despite the pain, had slept at home that night without medical treatment. Her arm was put in a cast and Viva recovered easily, showing that she matched her husband in hardiness.

R.C. Powell ran for sheriff and won easily. There was a sense of continuity as he took over from the man who had known him from childhood, who had trained him in law enforcement, and whose initials he even shared.

There was an old house in the Aldridge community that had belonged to Pace's uncle, John Pace, and his grandfather, Eli, before him. It was in the northeast part of the county near the Neches River. It was a simple, unpainted wood-frame place with a tin roof and a big porch in the front. John's son, Otho, raised his family there. When electricity came to the area, some Pace men took out their pistols and shot holes in the walls so the wires could be installed. The land around the house was good for a garden or for cattle and Pace was interested in both. Retirement was not a time to be lazy.

Just as his term ended, R.C. Pace learned that the Aldridge farm was for sale. His Uncle John's two daughters had no need to be so far from town. Pace had many happy memories of the place. It also desperately needed repairs. This made it an ideal project for a former carpenter. All he needed was the money.

Hardy loaned him what he needed and R.C. and Viva began to divide their time between the family home and Aldridge. Nothing about it was easy for Viva, who never learned to drive. She was sociable and had hoped that her husband's retirement would include travel. Instead, she found herself isolated, miles down dirt roads in a run-down farm.

R.C. could not have been happier. He bought cattle and kept his horse at the ready - saddled and tied to an oak tree in front of the house. He rebuilt the barn and he and Viva planted a small garden. His youngest son, Jimmy, was working out of state on oil pipeline projects. When he was in Jasper, he and his family stayed at the farm. This gave Viva's spirits a lift, because she had grandchildren to entertain and people who could give her a ride to town.

Even in his isolated corner of the county, Pace kept his hand in local politics. R.C. Powell, now sheriff, visited his old boss to discuss cases and problems on the job. Pace was a superior resource where there was a difficult political situation. Sheriff Powell had a deputy who was in some trouble. A local judge complained that this deputy and a female court employee were romantically involved. The deputy was married, so this created trouble for Sheriff Powell. The judge acted swiftly to fire the young woman and then confronted the sheriff, saying, "I got rid of the bitch. What are you going to do about the hound?" Pace told Powell he must get rid of the deputy or the scandal would be a liability in the next election. Powell took his counsel and asked the man to leave.

Back in Aldridge, R.C. repaired the smokehouse and made sausage. He also brewed some beer for his own enjoyment. While his life had none of the stresses and long hours of his career as sheriff, it was still full. People marveled that he did not grow "decrepit" in retirement. He entertained his grandchildren and often put them to work in his garden.

He briefly kept a mule at the farm. The animal was sickly and R.C. called Doc Miller, the local veterinarian, for help. When Miller arrived, he found the mule in poor shape. Pace's garden was another matter. Miller complimented R.C., saying, "I have never seen such a clean garden! There is not one blade of grass or one single weed here!" Pace just grinned and said, "Hell, I got me a good hoe!" Unfortunately, the mule did not respond to care as well as the garden. He developed bad diarrhea, or as the family called it, he "took scourers" and died.

In the summer of 1967, Pace and his youngest son enjoyed a bit of out of season deer hunting. Pace still had a taste for the young deer, "the younger the better" he joked. He had some trouble with one of his neighbors at that same time. The man, a Cajun named Guidry, had a reputation for cattle theft. There were local jokes about cows with a variety of brands that had found their way into Guidry's herd. Pace spent considerable time riding in his pasture, keeping lookout on his cows.

One day in early September, R.C. invited his sister, Beulah, to spend the night. Beulah still lived alone in her house on Milam Street. She was now eighty-two, and her brother was seventy-six. They sat in the swing on the front porch and reminisced that day. Both were still fairly active people. R.C. was relaxed and told her how glad he was that she could visit. He took his horse out again to protect his cattle. That evening, they all went to bed early.

Viva woke early the next morning and got up to make coffee. R.C. was lying across the bed with his leg bent and his ankle resting on one knee, in the familiar way he often sat in a chair. When Viva returned with coffee, she called to him. R.C. did not stir, and she quickly realized he was dead. She called to Beulah and then got on the phone to one of her daughters. Her son-in-law answered and she was able to tell him what happened. He notified Sheriff Powell and the rest of the family. They gathered quickly at the family home in town.

When Sheriff Powell arrived in Aldridge, he found R.C. stretched out on the bed. The scene was too peaceful, and R.C. looked too relaxed to be dead. Powell later said, "I would have brought him coffee, too." Most of the men who learned of the death insisted that it hit them a hard emotional blow, as if their own fathers had died. R.C. had meant so much to so many people in the town. Viva and the children began to plan the funeral. She called Joe Tonahill to serve as a pallbearer. Unfortunately, the attorney was in Mexico on a hunting trip, and could not be reached by phone. Some other young men who were fond of R.C. were also working out of the area at that time, and later expressed regret they had not been able to attend the funeral.

As he requested, R.C. was buried in the town cemetery and not in Peachtree. There was a large crowd at the funeral, and black and white residents joined in showing their respect for the former sheriff.

Viva returned to their home in town and remained there until poor health demanded that she move to a nursing home. She lived to the age of ninety. Beulah Pace Eddy lived to the age of one hundred. In her last years, she and Viva shared a room in the nursing home. The Pace family home and the farm at Aldridge are still owned by family members although no one lives in either place. Today, the three sons and three daughters of R.C. and Viva Pace all live in Jasper.

Afterword

The jail that R.C. Pace helped to build, and later worked in as sheriff, is now the home of the county historical archives. Much of the research material used in this book is housed there and I enjoyed hours of reading in my grandfather's old office as I worked on this book. Sheriff Powell served only a few terms and was followed by many different sheriffs, as Jasper voters became easily dissatisfied with a variety of men who served in that office. Powell later served as a county civil court judge until his death in 1998.

There are many people mentioned in this book and I attempted to find what became of some of them. Clayton Rushing was, of course, executed for the murders of his family, but his wife reportedly stayed in Newton County and remarried. Nothing was learned of the descendants of Josephine Elveston. The Garlington brothers lived away from town in later years and are now dead, as are most of the men involved in that case. Attempts were made to locate Clarence Willingham but they were not successful. The Garlington's sister, Leola, passed away in 2000 in Jasper. Wardlaw Lane, the Garlingtons' defense attorney, became a state judge. Attorney Joe Tonahill recently retired from his law practice in Jasper. He enjoyed fame from his defense of Jack Ruby, but had a long and very successful career in civil litigation, as well. Glen Faver, the attorney who shot Beaver Bishop in a supposed hunting accident, died in the 1970s. In his last years, he grew mentally confused and some people insisted that "he had Beaver Bishop on his conscience." Several of Pace's deputies still live in the Jasper area and I was able to interview them at length. Dr. Joe Dickerson, who accompanied Pace on the trip to Georgia to exhume the body of Roy Muench, still practices in Jasper.

Of R.C.'s children, only his son, Robert, entered county politics and has served as tax collector for many years. His son, Hardy, has a successful blueberry farm on the land at Aldridge.

In 1998, the town of Jasper became notorious for the first time since the Garlington shooting when a black man, James Byrd, was dragged to his death behind a pick-up truck by three young white men. The horror of the crime stirred up a lot of old hurts and fears and caused the community to unite in a surprising way to show the world that this crime was not all that Jasper was. The actions of the sheriff stood out as a good example of thorough and cooperative law enforcement. Many groups have justifiably honored Sheriff Billy Rowles for his work on that case.

Still, for those who want to portray the horror of the case as something common in the history of the town, the research does not prove this kind of cruelty and racism. At least over the period of R.C. Pace's tenure as sheriff, violent crime was mostly segregated. Black and white citizens, alike, faced the greatest threat of violence from their own family and friends. The one case that resulted in a death penalty conviction was that of Clayton Rushing. I found few cases in the county in which the perpetrator and victim were identified as being of different races. There was one case in a neighboring county where a black man who killed a white county official in a robbery received the death penalty. Brutal crimes such as stabbing or beating were invariably committed by family members.

This is not to say that there were no unreported crimes. Newspapers gave less and less information on violent crime as the years went on and if someone did not press charges from fear or intimidation, the historical record did not reflect it. For this, I have to fall back on the reputation that my grandfather had for pursuing criminals and being extremely knowledgeable about every part of the county he served. Since he left office, there have been murders in the county that have remained unsolved for years. It is not easy for a sheriff to combine the skills of a politician with those of a modern law enforcement officer. One former sheriff from the last decade was described to me as "the nicest fellow, who would tell anybody just what they wanted to hear," but then do nothing about crime. "He's a good old boy," one person said, "but WHAT is he good for?"

In a recent case, former resident Inez Wingfield and others killed a man in New Mexico, then brought the body to Jasper and buried it, perhaps believing that the county was a good place to hide a crime. Fortunately, the people involved could not keep quiet and tips led the local sheriff to discover the body. It still cannot be emphasized enough that the best weapon of law enforcement is information, and information is only shared when there is a relationship of trust between a community and its peace officers. Wingfield recently pled guilty in New Mexico to this brutal crime.

Some years ago one of Pace's grandchildren met a man who Pace had arrested the man long ago. The man did not remember the old sheriff warmly. Still, he described Pace in this way: " He was a mean old man, a mean old man. But he was good for his word."